Roger L. Dial

In Defense of
The American System

Our free trade agreements
have saved us so much money, we're broke.

Introduction

In Defense of
The American System

Roger L. Dial

Where's Papaw? Wrapped around the little fingers of Emmy Rae, Kylie Jo, Anna "Boochie", and Vivi Hope.

In Defense of The American System

In Defense of The American System

Introduction

What is the American System? Despite the newly created Federal Reserve collapsing the dollar's value, followed by the Great Depression, and the American System being dismantled in 1913, American manufacturing was largely unchallenged by foreign competition leading up to World War II. This was due in no small part to the recovery effort underway among our future competitor nations that had suffered heavy losses to their manufacturing infrastructure during World War I. After World War II, our competitors were once again in rebuilding mode which for the most part, kept their products from competing with American manufacturers well into the fifties.

The benefits of domestic industry weren't wholly undone until the advent of the North American Free Trade Agreement along with Asian trade agreements. These reduced us from a nation of producers competing on similar terms on the global stage, to a wrecked manufacturing sector whose scapegoat was the American worker who could not hope to compete with the pennies per hour paid to foreign laborers, or worse, slave laborers.

In the production run-up to the Second World War when factories of all types were converting over to the war effort, production men applied innovative ideas to an issue that up to that point wasn't recognized as a problem. A Frigidaire factory converted over to making Browning 50 caliber machine guns. They took what had previously been a largely handmade operation and applied the ideas and suggestions from the people actually building the guns. The result of their modern manufacturing methods increased the firing rate of the gun, improved quality, and increased production to five times that of the original schedule with only twice as many machines and people at only 25% of the original cost. The total of all their ideas revolutionized machine gun manufacturing.

Consider the teamwork and innovation that took place between factory personnel that were vested in the outcome and quality of the products they produced compared to low wage or forced slave laborers that make most of the products we use today. We've been sold the notion that by cheapening our costs of production through low wage workers in third world and communist countries, that we have increased our purchasing power. But, consumers and taxpayers are only a renewable resource as long their ability to produce is not exported to a foreign country. For every job lost in the manufacturing sector, 1.4 additional jobs dependent on that manufacturing are also lost according to the Bureau of Labor Statistics.

Now take as an example two companies making the

same product but using different business strategies. One company CEO is involved in every aspect of his company. His competitor however, relies on the opinion of advisors repeating what they learned in school from reading Adam Smith's treatise on the British System of free trade economics.

Chances are, these college educated captains of industry have essentially been given two choices in their studies. They've likely weighed the points of Marxism vs. Free Trade without ever having the benefit of properly studying the American System that was the economic foundation of the United States for no less than 124 years.

The free trade company owner has a bean counter who, though he is gifted at counting beans, has no understanding of the importance of dialogue between the engineer who designs the product for assembly, and the factory worker that must assemble the product. The designer works entirely from a computer using "Theoretical Knowledge" with no practical work experience. The product is functional but complicated to assemble. The bean counter has assured the company owner that he can make more money using Chinese labor. But the engineers can't dialogue with the Chinese factory because they don't speak Mandarin. The dirt wage Chinese worker isn't vested in the product or the efficiency of its design, so he assembles it as is. The product arrives back in the states and it works, so it's deemed a success despite the international shipping charges, customs, and lack of turnaround time on design changes, modifications, and defects.

Now consider the company owner that is involved in every aspect of his company and the product he sells. His bean counter tries to sell him on cheap Chinese labor but he investigates further.

The engineer designs everything using computer aided design and operates strictly from "Theoretical Knowledge". The factory worker relies on spatial reasoning and awareness developed from "Practical Knowledge".

The American factory worker looks at the design and sees what a mess it is to assemble. The engineer and the factory worker put their heads together and it makes a funny sound called English. They combine theoretical knowledge with practical knowledge and improve the design thereby improving the efficiency of the build, and the quality of the product. The domestic manufacturer decides to go with domestic production and is actually able to sell his superior product cheaper than his overseas producing competitor and is able to get his product from the assembly line to the consumer in a day or so versus a month or more. (1)

The American System evolved under Henry Clay from Alexander Hamilton's American School of

Economics. It consisted of three mutually reinforcing parts; a tariff to protect and promote American industry; a national bank to encourage commerce; and federal subsidies for national improvements like roads and canals to develop agriculture and manufacturing.

The American System came into being after the war of 1812. The re-charter for the national bank failed to pass in 1811, leaving the country with virtually no means to finance the war which left the nation deeply in debt. The Treasury was in default; Congress was incapable of securing financing, and the government was essentially bankrupt. The nation's debt was over 127 million dollars. After the implementation of the American System, the national debt was extinguished by 1835 without income or payroll taxes. This was accomplished with a population less than 2.5% the size of America in the 21st century. The annual per capita income for this time period averaged one hundred dollars per worker.

The period of seven years prior to the Tariff of 1824 was up to that time, generally felt to be the most dismal since the Constitution was established. The Tariff of 1816 was making progress toward paying off our crippling debt from two wars but eight years later, it was still over 90 million dollars. Property values were at their lowest since the depression began. Commerce and navigation were threatened with complete paralysis. Desperate and ruined people were taking terrible losses on the sale of real estate. Property values in New York fell by nearly six million dollars. Senator Clay said that if he had to pick any period since the Constitution was adopted, that exhibited the most widespread dismay and desolation; it would be the seven years which immediately preceded the Tariff of 1824.

Following passage of the Tariff of 1824, employment came back until the nation was fully and profitably employed; property values increased; cities were expanding and villages were springing up. Property values in New York rebounded and grew by 44 million dollars. Our interior rivers were perpetually busy with the traffic of steamboats. Our exports and imports were increased and rising. The treasury was overflowing and Congress was looking for items to eliminate taxes from instead of looking for new ways to tax and raise revenue. Senator Clay said that if he were to select any period of the greatest prosperity since the establishment of our Constitution, it would be the period of seven years immediately following passage of the Tariff of 1824.

"On a general survey, we behold cultivation extended, the arts flourishing, the face of the country improved, our people fully and profitably employed, and the public countenance exhibiting tranquility, contentment, and happiness: And, if we descend into particulars, we have the

agreeable contemplation of a people out of debt; land rising slowly in value, but in a secure and salutary degree; a ready, though not extravagant market for all the surplus productions of our industry; innumerable flocks and herds browsing and gamboling on ten thousand hills and plains, covered with rich and verdant grasses; our cities expanded, and whole villages springing up, as it were, by enchantment; our exports and imports increased and increasing; our tonnage, foreign and coastwise, swelling and fully occupied; the rivers of our interior animated by the perpetual thunder and lightning of countless steamboats; the currency sound and abundant; the public debt of two wars nearly redeemed; and, to crown all, the public treasury overflowing, embarrassing Congress, not to find subjects of taxation, but to select the objects which shall be liberated from the impost. If the term of seven years were to be selected of the greatest prosperity which this people have enjoyed since the establishment of their present Constitution, it would be exactly that period of seven years which immediately followed the passage of the tariff of 1824."(2)

To date, Senator Ted Cruz is the only presidential candidate that has put forth a plan that would tie our currency to a stable level of gold. The plan would eliminate the income tax, payroll tax, death tax, and abolish the IRS. All individuals making over $36,000 a year would pay a 10% flat tax. Mortgage and charitable contributions would still be deductible. The business tax would be 16% across the board. Imports would be taxed at the corporate level of 16% but exporters would be exempt. That's not as high as the tariff of 1816, but an order of magnitude better than what we have now. That would put us as close as we've been to the American System since 1913—provided Cruz doesn't give a pass to importers posing as exporters, but who in fact are only repackaging imported goods for export.

Simply put, the American System creates jobs in America which helps everyone including American companies—because a company can't survive if they export the jobs of all their customers.

It's not a theory; it's history, and the American System powered this nation for over half its existence. A lot of people probably feel like they live in the wrong half.

***

In Defense of The American System

Chapter 1 The Greatest Alexander

When President Lincoln heard complaints that General Ulysses S. Grant was drinking alcohol to excess, his response was, "Find out what Grant drinks and send a barrel of it to each of my other generals!"

The number one epithet hurled at Alexander Hamilton by his foes who could never hope to defeat him on the field of debate, was that he was a bastard—literally. If bastard birth is what made Alexander Hamilton the man that he was, then may we be a Bastardom, and Alexander Hamilton the King of Bastards.

Alexander Hamilton's economic model was so brilliant in concept, that despite his early death, the American School of economics lived on, with no small help from Henry Clay, and catapulted the United States past Great Britain for America's standard of living and quality of life. His model was the economic engine of America for no less than 124 years before being mortally wounded by the Federal Reserve, global free trade, and their requisite life support system of income tax, payroll tax, devalued currency, and a forced labor slave workforce. It lived 16 more years before dying in 1929, though it can be contended that it survived into the 1990's.

To say that slavery was the farthest consideration from Alexander Hamilton's mind while crafting the economic policy that would catapult the United States past every nation on earth would be an understatement; it was never a consideration. Though the scourge of slavery would cling tenaciously to our landscape, the American System created an atmosphere that slavery could not survive in, and eventually resulted in the Civil War. Many historians rightly claim the Civil War was about free trade and taxation, for slavery is the hidden linchpin of a free trade economy and requires direct taxation through income taxes of its citizens. The American System on the other hand met the needs of our nation without income and payroll taxes.

By contrast, the role of slavery was pivotal in the free trade economic policy of Adam Smith which is revered and taught by virtually every notable economist of the last 200 years.

Alexander Hamilton's plan for American prosperity was economic independence as a nation. Adam Smith's economic plan extolled the virtue and use of slavery where appropriate. Hamilton's writings have been declared foolish, and xenophobic, while Smith's is taught as the proper path to economic freedom.

Alexander Hamilton believed in America's independence as an economy as much as he believed in our independence as a nation. Slavery was not a consideration in his policy for America's economic freedom. Slavery is never mentioned in his economic policy, "Report on Manufactures".

By contrast, Adam Smith, the father of free trade and author of "Wealth of Nations", lays out his recipe for colonialism and details how slavery can achieve the greatest benefits in an economy, as well as some of the drawbacks. The relevance of slavery to a free trade economy is referenced no less than 75 times in his opus, Wealth of Nations.

As summarized by Dr. Peter Soderbaum of Malardalen University, Sweden, "This neoclassical trade theory focuses on one dimension, i.e., the price at which a commodity can be delivered, and is extremely narrow in cutting off a large number of other considerations about impacts on employment in different parts of the world, about environmental impacts and on culture." (1)

Here are some thoughts from the founding father of free trade who is the icon for nine out of ten modern economists, Adam Smith:

"A laborer, it may be said, indeed, ought to save part of his summer wages, in order to defray his winter expense; and that, through the whole year, they do not exceed what is necessary to maintain his family through the whole year. A slave, however, or one absolutely dependent on us for immediate subsistence, would not be treated in this manner. His daily subsistence would be proportioned to his daily necessities." (2)

"The profits of a tobacco plantation, though inferior to those of sugar, are superior to those of corn, as has already been observed. Both can afford the expense of slave cultivation but sugar can afford it still better than tobacco. The number of Negroes, accordingly, is much greater, in proportion to that of whites, in our sugar than in our tobacco colonies." (3)

"The pride of man makes him love to domineer, and nothing mortifies him so much as to be obliged to condescend to persuade his inferiors. Wherever the law allows it, and the nature of the work can afford it, therefore, he will generally prefer the service of slaves to that of freemen." (4)

"The planting of sugar and tobacco can afford the expense of slave cultivation. The raising of corn, it seems, in the present times, cannot." (5)

"Among the ancient Romans, the lands of the rich were all cultivated by slaves, who wrought under an overseer, who was likewise a slave; so that a poor freeman had little chance of being employed either as a farmer or as a laborer." (6)

"Rum is a very important article in the trade which the Americans carry on to the coast of Africa, from which they bring back Negro slaves in return." (7)

"It is in the progress of the North American colonies, however, that the superiority of the English policy chiefly appears. The progress of the sugar colonies of France has been at least equal, perhaps superior, to that of the greater part of those of England; and yet the sugar colonies of England enjoy a free government, nearly of the same kind with that which takes place in her colonies of North America. But the sugar colonies of France are not discouraged, like those of England, from refining their own sugar; and what is still of greater importance, the genius of their government naturally introduces a better management of their Negro slaves." (8)

"In every country where the unfortunate law of slavery is established, the magistrate, when he protects the slave, intermeddles in some measure in the management of the private property of the master." (9)

"Gentle usage renders the slave not only more faithful, but more intelligent, and, therefore, upon a double account, more useful." (10)

"The blacks, indeed, who make the greater part of the inhabitants, both of the southern colonies upon the (North American) continent and of the West India islands, as they are in a state of slavery, are, no doubt, in a worse condition than the poorest people either in Scotland or Ireland. We must not, however, upon that account, imagine that they are worse fed, or that their consumption of articles which might be subjected to moderate duties, is less than that even of the lower ranks of people in England. In order that they may work well, it is the interest of their master that they should be fed well, and kept in good heart, in the same manner as it is his interest that his working cattle should be so." (11)

Why does slavery factor so heavily in global free trade? Free trade globally is untenable without forced labor slavery, though any of the current 27 million slaves that feed our global supply chain would appreciate it if free trade advocates would prove otherwise. Free trade within the borders of a free nation, as Alexander Hamilton designed and Henry Clay championed, fosters competition, innovation, progress, prosperity, and economic freedom.

Few could grasp, in his time or since, concepts that Alexander Hamilton, at barely 30 years of age, could accurately see as future consequence relative to current events. He saw the potential peril that bills of rights could be to the Constitution, and laid out scenarios we're seeing played out two and a quarter centuries later, while others are just now beginning to grasp the folly of those who conspire to redefine the Bill of Rights. He admonished advocates of the amendments that bills of rights would open dangerous debates by hinting that government had power to restrict liberties where no power existed to the government to impose restrictions on any liberty. Those like Jefferson, and many others who were most opposed to a powerful central government, arguably had noble intentions, yet helped lay the foundation for government to dare to believe they had power that was never granted, nor the founding fathers ever intended.

Alexander Hamilton viewed bills of rights as a peril that would invite future tyrants to challenge, manipulate and jeopardize our liberties, while claiming powers they were never granted. He said:

I go further, and affirm that bills of rights, in the sense and to the extent in which they are contended for, are not only unnecessary in the proposed Constitution, but would even be dangerous. They would contain various exceptions to powers not granted; and, on this very account, would afford a colorable pretext to claim more than were granted. For why declare that things shall not be done which there is no power to do? Why, for instance, should it be said that the liberty of the press shall not be restrained, when no power is given by which restrictions may be imposed? I will not contend that such a provision would confer a regulating power; but it is evident that it would furnish, to men disposed to usurp, a plausible pretense for claiming that power. They might urge with a semblance of reason, that the Constitution ought not to be charged with the absurdity of providing against the abuse of an authority which was not given, and that the provision against restraining the liberty of the press afforded a clear implication, that a power to prescribe proper regulations concerning it was intended to be vested in the national government. This may serve as a specimen of the numerous handles which would be given to the doctrine of constructive powers, by the indulgence of an injudicious zeal for bills of rights.— Alexander Hamilton, Federalist No. 84.

Thomas Jefferson opposed a federal government, though his intentions may have been noble, he lacked the foresight to see this nation as more than a farming society, which opposed Alexander Hamilton's vision of America as an agricultural *and* industrial juggernaut. Jefferson, by demanding bills of rights be added to the Constitution, ceded imaginary powers to the government where no power previously existed; the power to trample liberties.

Thomas Jefferson also thought the Constitution should expire after a generation. He proposed that the Constitution expire every nineteen years. Once Jefferson came to terms with the problems associated with it, he relented. Jefferson is revered, but Alexander Hamilton is to this day excoriated for putting forth the suggestion of lifetime appointments for the President, with the exception of being removed from office for bad behavior. Hamilton was labeled a Monarchist. That's why it was called a Constitutional *Convention*. Singularly, many of the drafters of the Constitution were at times "out of step", but as a convention, they created a magnificent document. There was no greater champion for the struggle to ratify the Constitution than Alexander Hamilton.

Alexander Hamilton, brought forth at the age of 30, the most authoritative interpretation of the Constitution for the greatest system of government ever conceived, and when finished, proceeded to create the greatest economic model of any nation on earth; an economic model that survived his untimely death by no less than 104 years—withstanding assault by free trade zealots; small, petty, stealers of men, who would throw our borders open wide for foreign nations to recolonize the Union, in the name of a one dimensional philosophy, Free Trade—that gives no regard for national employment, sovereignty, the environment, or the sustainability of a consumer base stripped of its manufacturing capabilities. Were that not enough, he went on as Secretary of the Treasury to create a national bank whose mission was to issue debt free, precious metal backed currency, and encourage the domestic economy with sovereign powers to regulate credit and encourage the development of domestic commerce and industry while preventing the export of money. That is the biased and true synopsis of Alexander Hamilton.

Modern politicians, historians, pundits and especially economists attempt to paint Alexander Hamilton as the inventor of the Federal Reserve System. Blaming

Alexander Hamilton for the Federal Reserve is like blaming Gottfried J. Schmidt for the 9/11 terrorist attacks. Gottfried J. Schmidt invented the box cutter in the 1930s'.

He was all but technically an orphan at age 11, and lived with his mother's relatives before going to work for a West Indian merchant at the age of 13. He was so self-reliant that he was left in charge as head of the business when the owner was away. Relatives and friends, such as Presbyterian minister, Rev. Hugh Knox were determined to cultivate his enormous potential and sent him to Boston to attend grammar school. He arrived in America from the island of Nevis, in the West Indies when he was 15 years old in October, 1772. (12)

Being new to America, he had no attachments to the Colonials or Great Britain and had to make up his own mind as he struggled initially on which side to take. A meeting was held in what is now known as City Hall Park in New York City on July 6, 1774, to advocate joining other colonies in calling a Congress. Hamilton, only 17, attended, and became increasingly frustrated while listening to the speeches because of what was *not* being said. He was received enthusiastically after he worked his way through the crowd to the platform and gave his argument for the colonial side. By March 1, 1777, Washington offered Hamilton the rank of Lieutenant-Colonel to be on his staff at merely 20 years of age. (13)

He addressed a letter in 1780, at age 23 to a member of Congress, detailing a remarkable analysis of the defects of the Articles of Confederation, and the same year he sent letters to Robert Morris, the future head of the Treasury Department, and discussed paper currency and the causes of its depreciation. He proposed to restore solvency to the nation by gradually contracting the volume of paper currency, taxes and foreign loans, which was to form the basis of a national bank. (14)

Hamilton studied law for 4 months at age 25 and passed the bar, but soon accepted a position from Robert Morris as a continental receiver of taxes for New York. He set forth drafting resolutions that would give Congress power to provide revenue. He believed the central government should be responsible for the war debts incurred by the states. (15)

During the Philadelphia Convention in 1787, Hamilton, age 30, gave a six hour speech when it was proposed that the Constitution should be formed by revising the old Articles of Confederation. He expressed the Union's need to "adopt a solid plan without regard to temporary opinions." Hamilton was neither supportive of a fully republican form of government nor fully democratic, but said, "I acknowledge I do not think favorably of republican government; but I address my remarks to those who do, in order to prevail on them to tone their government as high as possible. I profess myself as zealous an advocate for liberty as any man whatever, and trust I shall be as willing a martyr to it, though I differ as to the form in which it is most eligible. Real liberty is neither found in despotism nor in the extremes of democracy, but in moderate governments. Those who mean to form a solid republic ought to proceed to the confines of another government. If we incline too much to democracy, we shall soon shoot into a monarchy... It is essential to the democratic rights of the community that the first branch be directly elected by the people."

Hamilton entered the fray again during the convention when the proposal was put forth to grant the government power to print unfunded paper currency, not backed by silver or gold, but on the nation's credit. He vigorously opposed government authority to issue unfunded paper currency as a substitute for gold and silver. (16)

While traveling from the Philadelphia Convention, back to New York, Hamilton began writing arguments based on the points of opposition to the Constitution. There would be eighty-five such letters written and sent to newspapers over the next twenty weeks. Hamilton wrote fifty-one letters and enlisted the aid of James Madison and John Jay to write others. Hamilton collaborated on twenty of their letters for a total input of seventy-one of the eighty-five essays that became known as the proper interpretation and exposition of constitutional law, "The Federalist".

The Constitution became the supreme law of the United States and went into effect on March 4, 1789. President George Washington was inaugurated April 30, 1789 and appointed Alexander Hamilton as the nation's first Secretary of the Treasury. Within ten days of his appointment, Congress requested a report on the public credit, including the collection and management of revenue, receipts and expenditures, and the regulation of currency. When Congress convened in January, he submitted his report, "On Public Credit". At this time, economic science wasn't young; it was in its newborn infancy, yet Hamilton's economic model would be the cornerstone of American finance for the next one-hundred-twenty-four years.

Revisionists, anti-Federalist and the uninformed, who justifiably revile the speculative practices and institution of the Federal Reserve, blame Alexander Hamilton for its creation because he created the first national bank. The Federal Reserve bears as much resemblance to the banking system of Alexander Hamilton as black does to white. Hamilton vehemently opposed unfunded currency not backed by gold and silver. He was equally opposed to inflationary and high risk speculative banking practices like that of the Federal Reserve. Hamilton affirmed that a nation with sound credit would prevent the export of money. In contrast, free trade and the Federal Reserve has put America's credit rating in peril while devalued currency and manufacturers are fleeing our shores.

The national bank instituted by Hamilton was so successful in restoring the national credit, that President George Washington wrote, "Our public credit stands on that ground, which, three years ago, it would have been madness to have foretold. The astonishing rapidity with which the newly instituted bank was filled, gives an unexampled proof of the resources of our countrymen and their confidence in public measures. On the first day of opening the subscription, the whole number of shares (twenty thousand) were taken up in one hour, and application made for upwards of four thousand shares more than were granted by the institution, besides many others that were coming in from various quarters." (17)

The bank's charter expired in 1811 and a new charter was voted on in the House, but not acted on in the Senate, eventually resulting in the defeat of the re-charter. War broke out the following year in the War of 1812, and left the nation struggling to raise money to fund the war. This was the only period from 1800 to 1913, that the value of our dollar's buying power dropped below 100 cents, where it otherwise averaged $1.60 for one-hundred-thirteen years, until the Federal Reserve and the precipitous decline of the dollar began, meaning, the economic status of owning $1.00 in 1900 is equivalent to owning $204.00 in 2013. (18)

Today we read and hear how difficult it is to get our products into countries that we want to sell to. Our ports are open to the influx of products from all over the world, but what port freely admits our surplus?

In 1791, Alexander Hamilton published his report on manufactures. Other than the language used and some of the industries referenced, the dilemma facing our founders for getting American goods to a global market were the same then as they are now.

America's focus at that time was import/export. We relied heavily on imports of finished products in exchange for the raw materials we produced and exported. Our manufacturing industry was in its infancy and unable to compete with foreign manufacturers, yet the ports of these foreign countries were heavily regulated against our products thereby preventing our entry into their markets—just like today.

Alexander Hamilton was able to see the problem and formulate a remedy when he wrote to Congress on December 5, 1791. The following is a paragraph from

Alexander Hamilton's letter to Congress explained in modern English. It is followed by the actual text from his report, so that you can judge the veracity of my interpretation.

"The importance of encouraging manufacturing in the United States, which not long ago seemed not so important, appears to be generally understood by everyone now. The embarrassments that have obstructed our exports have led to serious consideration on the necessity of improving our domestic industry. The restrictive regulations from foreign markets that hinder the export of our increasing surplus of agricultural produce, serves to cause a sincere desire that a more extensive demand for that surplus may be created here at home, and have complete success like some already valuable sections of our manufacturing sector. This will be accompanied by the inevitable criticism from less mature opinions, but in others, it will justify a hope, that the obstacles to the growth of this segment of industry are not as formidable as they were thought to be. It will not be difficult to find, that if this policy is extended further, full compensation will be had for any disadvantages suffered from outside influences. Also, we will have attained resources that are beneficial to our national independence and safety."(19)

"The expediency of encouraging manufactures in the

United States, which was not long since deemed very questionable, appears at this time to be pretty generally admitted. The embarrassments, which have obstructed the progress of our external trade, have led to serious reflections on the necessity of enlarging the sphere of our domestic commerce: the restrictive regulations, which in foreign markets abridge the vent of the increasing surplus of our Agricultural produce, serve to beget an earnest desire, that a more extensive demand for that surplus may be created at home: And the complete success, which has rewarded manufacturing enterprise, in some valuable branches, conspiring with the promising symptoms, which attend some less mature essays, in others, justify a hope, that the obstacles to the growth of this species of industry are less formidable than they were apprehended to be; and that it is not difficult to find, in its further extension; a full indemnification for any external disadvantages, which are or may be experienced, as well as an accession of resources, favourable to national independence and safety."(20)

When there was need for an enduring government model, Alexander Hamilton was the champion that delivered ratification for the Constitution. He delivered again, setting the nation on course as an industrial superpower with his economic policy, the American School. He designed a banking system that issued debt free, precious metal backed currency, encouraged the domestic economy, with sovereign power to regulate credit and encourage the development of domestic commerce and industry through a strong dollar, while steering clear of the speculative banking practices that the U.S. falls victim to today.

***

In Defense of The American System

Chapter 2 The Law of Comparative Advantage

Why does the leadership of the Republican, Libertarian, and Democrat Party support free trade? Look first at the definition of free trade and you'll see that it is a policy by which a government does not discriminate against imports or interfere with exports by applying tariffs to imports, or subsidies to exports and quotas. According to the law of comparative advantage, the policy permits mutual gains from the trade of goods and services to trading partners.

Here is an analogous explanation of free trade or more specifically, the law of comparative advantage.

You have a job making $300 per day and your child has a car that needs brakes. It will cost $100 to install new brakes but you can do the job yourself for half that price, so you miss work to fix the brakes. The parts cost $50 and you fix the car. If you missed the entire work day, the $50 brake job cost you $350, the same as if you had worked and overpaid a mechanic by $250.

The law of comparative advantage would logically dictate that you (America) go to work and make $300, pay the mechanic (China) $100 and come away with a $200 profit instead of doing the job yourself. The mechanic has the comparative advantage because he can do the job for you $250 cheaper than you can do the job yourself.

Have I sold you on the logic of Free Trade and the superiority of the law of comparative advantage? I hope not, although that is the lie that has been foisted on Americans for hundreds of years. The law of comparative advantage works brilliantly for all Americans when free trade takes place between free Americans. When a large American corporation decides it's cheaper to sub-contract parts production to an American small business, everybody wins and domestic productivity increases.

The brake job example of comparative advantage is an apple to apple comparison. The law of comparative advantage as it relates to global free trade is like comparing apples to asteroids for American labor. The average hourly compensation package in 2011 for American manufacturing is $35.53 compared to $1.88 for China, yes, one dollar and eighty-eight pennies.

When comparative advantage takes place within our borders, a manufacturing worker might lose his job to an innovative sub-contractor who can do the work cheaper and/or more efficiently. He has at worst, an opportunity to find a job with a sub-contractor in his line of work and take a pay and/or benefit cut. If the sub-contractor is cheaper because of his innovation and efficiency, the workers might well be paid more than when they worked for the contractor directly.

However, an American worker is not going to move

his family to China for a compensation package of $1.88 per hour, or to Bangladesh where the minimum wage is $0.18 per hour. When multi-national corporations repeat this process enough times, there are scarce few jobs left in America that haven't been outsourced to cheap foreign sweat shop labor. What Americans are left with are low paying jobs in the service industry.

China has been accused of being a currency manipulator, but maybe American labor is an apple to apple comparison to Chinese labor after all. Before the Federal Reserve and its speculative practices replaced the National Bank in 1913, the U.S. dollar had the buying power of $1.75. Multiply that times $35.53 and compensation for American manufacturing should be equivalent to $62.17. Unfortunately, since the Federal Reserve took over our money supply, the dollar's value has dropped from $1.75 in 1913 to $0.05 or less today which is a nickel compared to 1913. A compensation package of $35.53 per hour in 2011 is only worth $1.77 now compared to its value before the Fed took over in 1913. Gee, we really can do it cheaper than the Chinese.

That is of course, a completely false comparison because the world's currency is tied to the American dollar *now* and not what the American dollar *used* to be, meaning, if $35.53 in 1913, is worth $1.77 now, then China's $1.88 would be worth $0.13.

The Federal Reserve has repeatedly lowered the value of our currency to compete in the global market. Every time we lower the worth of our currency to compete, foreign competitors lower theirs. The American dollar is virtually worthless now.

The dollar's value briefly dropped to $0.93 during the War of 1812; otherwise the dollar has never been worth less than one hundred copper pennies from 1800 until 1913. When the Federal Reserve took over, the dollar went over the cliff and lost 92% of its value from 1913 to 1920.

Can you imagine living in a country whose dollar buying power averaged no less than $1.60 for one hundred thirteen years? That was the United States from 1800 until 1913. If a man bought a horse in 1800 for $50, his great, great grandchildren could buy an identical horse in 1900 for $25. However, his great, great, great, great grandchildren would have to pay $500 for an identical horse in 2000. $50,000 in 1800 had the buying power of $1,000,000 in 2012. $50,000 in 1900 had the buying power of $2,000,000 in 2012.

Free trade hucksters would have you believe that our current version of free trade fosters innovation and competition when in fact it has exactly the opposite effect. The current version of free trade that has been dumped on America is nothing more than American corporations fleeing from their competitors and the innovation wrought by free Americans competing against free Americans. They scurry to low-tech third world and/or communist countries to produce their wares in crumbling infrastructure with antiquated machinery while using dirt wage or worse, a forced slave labor work force.

There is no competition under the system that we live under now; not one that most can benefit from; not one that most can compete in as a participant; and why? Our field of play has been taken away. If you're a blue collar American with a job that's not tied somehow to the federal government, then you quite possibly don't have a job, or don't have the job you used to have, or don't have a job that you feel like you can safely retire from.

Politicians who are bought and paid for either by foreign corporations or American corporations operating in foreign lands enjoy nothing more than talking about small businesses and how the other side of the political aisle is destroying your chance at the American dream because they're making it so hard for the average American to start their own business.

When I think of small business, and I mean small business as it once was, I think of big business. There is no small business without big business. Small business without big business is a flower shop, a crafts store, or a repair shop, although we've been told for so long that repairs on the cheap foreign products we buy are so expensive that it would be cheaper to buy a new one, so we don't even bother to see if our products can be repaired anymore. We buy Chinese products; we break them; we kick them to the curb and go buy another.

America's economic sovereignty is long since forfeited. Of the few things we still produce in this country, energy is one. The Saudis, while sitting on vast cash reserves, courtesy of our own ineptitude, are waging war on the U.S. by glutting the market, and brilliantly too I would add. The United States is the largest oil producer in the world now and the Saudis want their market share back. An often heard quip is "oil producing nations". America is *not* an oil producing nation; America is a nation of oil producing companies. Saudi Arabia is an oil producing nation and they have declared war on American drilling.

The same politicians that push for international free trade agreements in order to placate the lobbyists they are in indebted to are hypocrites who don't even support free markets within the United States.

Minimum wage for instance has been used as an underhanded tactic to price competition out of the market by states attempting to skirt around illegal interstate trade tariffs. Northern states with high labor costs may push for an increase in national minimum wage laws as a means to protect themselves from lower wage labor in southern industries.

Here's a hypothetical example. Consider a lobbyist for a textile industry in New York that has an average wage rate of $18 an hour and is getting hammered by competition in South Carolina with an average wage rate of $12 an hour.

A lobbyist yanks a leash and tells his politician to, "Sic'em!" If the New York politician pushes for a state increase in minimum wage, he hasn't helped his cause—but—if he successfully manages to get a federal minimum wage increase to $15 an hour, he has just successfully landed a damaging blow to his southern competitor, where state residents have a much lower cost of living than their metropolitan competition . This is one way politicians get around illegal interstate tariffs—by pushing for a wage that is already lower than the average for workers in their own state, but higher than in the competitive state that they want to put out of business.

Some individual states are raising their minimum wage and I think it's wonderful. As the resident of a state with the second lowest cost of living in America, I hope surrounding states raise their minimum wage to $20 an hour. Then their industries can come to my state and put people to work.

When the Utica Shale was discovered in Ohio with potentially vast reserves of oil and natural gas, Republican Governor John Kasich said, "I don't want foreigners working on our drill rigs. And foreigners are people from Pennsylvania, West Virginia, Kentucky and Indiana." This guy is one of free trade's biggest cheerleaders but he doesn't even support free markets within the borders of his own nation. I guess it's not free trade when it's free Americans competing against other free Americans.

Interstate protectionism within the United States is as harmful to Americans as global free trade. It is rightly why a protection tariff between states is declared illegal by the U.S. Constitution.

Free markets are a beautiful thing—but what is a free market? Competing gas stations across the street from each other in a price war and lowering prices in order to compete for customers is the beauty of the free market at work.

Competing drilling companies submitting their best offer for a drilling contract and hoping theirs is the winning bid is the beauty of the free market.

What is not a free market is when foreign predator nations like those in OPEC, whose nationalized oil industries—with malice, and premeditation, set out to bankrupt an entire nation of individual companies. The loss of our domestic energy sector threatens our national independence and safety. We philosophize away our domestic industry and hold the door open wide for nations that at the basest level, despise us and wish to do us harm.

When I was young and did something wasteful, my

father would often make me dig a hole and fill it back up to teach me a lesson about the futility of waste. I had to dig more than a few holes, so many in fact that I made a life's work of finding ways to make digging holes a productive endeavor. I now dig holes and fill them back up with cement and steel, from which come oil and gas. Small businesses are made possible by people who make things and the thing I make best is a hole in the ground.

When my ability to make holes is interrupted by a foreign government's interference like Saudi Arabia, more than the sixteen or so men under my employ are affected. How many people directly lose their job on a drilling rig in the aftermath of Saudi Arabia's attack on America's drilling industry? Saudi Arabia and the rest of OPEC are attacking us in an attempt to gain back the market share they lost to our innovations. One hundred people lose their job immediately between the two rigs used to drill the hole and this doesn't include the army of workers who come after the hole is drilled to complete the well and get the gas to your home, business or power plant.

When our drilling program was halted, fourteen small businesses lost their livelihood because their existence depended on a big business. Add to that the businesses that felt the immediate impact of our departure such as motels, pipe yards, cementing services, ISPs', on-site housing rental, truck drivers, drilling supply stores, restaurants, grocery stores, etc. Add to that list the scores of pipeline workers, heavy equipment operators, safety flaggers, fuel deliveries, coal miners who migrated into oil and gas mining because President Obama kept his promise and bankrupted their industry, more trucking, more motels and more etc.

Now—exactly what small business do these people start after they've invested capital and sweat into their small businesses? What do they do after they've packed up and gone home because our government rolled over when a foreign predator declared war on an entire American industry?

As a former software developer for combat flight simulators, general aviation simulators and real aviation packages for flight schools, I understand a little about what it takes to get a product from idea to design and eventually to market. President Obama has a plan for the common man to overthrow China with a computer and a 3D printer.

President Obama suggests these displaced workers take a course in 3D printer design and operation which has absolutely no economy of scale. They can buy a 3D printer and either make a computer model of their own design, which is a daunting task in a field which only the most accomplished can stay abreast. Another alternative is to browse online for user made models that can be purchased, but none of these can be mass produced on a 3D printer because they're just too slow. A 3D printer, which by the way is touted as the obsolescence of China—can only achieve economy of scale if the 3D printer is used to design a prototype made usually out of plastic or polymer. The designer must then acquire access to a factory, most likely in China, to mass produce his invention. If mass production is not a viable option, the user is shackled by very limited output that will be sold as tchotchke on E-bay. If the design for their product is purchased online and not custom, all propriety advantage is lost.

I hear politicians speak of small business in our current economic environment and what comes to mind are not sub-contracting businesses participating as a vital link in the supply chain of industry, but instead I think of small cottage businesses.

Why Free Trade? Proponents pitch it to us, the unwashed masses as a policy we can't refuse. Does anyone in America still believe that the benefit of low prices on foreign imports exceed the harm that has been done to our domestic industry, unemployment, swelling welfare rolls and calls for higher taxes to support a population that is increasing in government dependence?

Is personal resignation or compromise the result of seeing no way out, or worse; attempting to accommodate and adjust to the global free trade premise that as an experiment is a complete failure?

Would you rather a product be cheap because you can afford it with your shrinking paycheck or would you rather a product be cheap because you have a good job and can afford to buy what you want?

Free trade cheapens a product because the producer of the product is cheap. The American System cheapens a product because it elevates the producer of the product.

I have long said that I would rather pay $100 for something when I can afford it than $50 for something when I cannot. The facts prove that historically, the American System has the opposite effect and does not increase the cost of goods and services, but in fact decreases the costs of goods and services, through competition and innovation.

Protectionism (The American System) is portrayed as the antithesis to free trade when in fact, the American System was the purest working example of free trade ever established.

President William McKinley, a staunch protector of domestic industry, if not overzealous, said, "They say, if you had not had the Protective Tariff things would be a little cheaper. Well, whether a thing is cheap or dear depends upon what we can earn by our daily labor. Free trade cheapens the product by cheapening the producer. Protection cheapens the product by elevating the producer. Under free trade the trader is the master and the producer the slave. Protection is but the law of nature, the law of self-preservation, of self-development, of securing the highest and best destiny of the race of man."

He also said, "Well, they say, 'Buy where you can buy the cheapest'.... Of course, that applies to labor as to everything else. Let me give you a maxim that is a thousand times better than that and it is the protection maxim: 'buy where you can pay the easiest.' And that spot of earth is where labor wins its highest rewards." (1)

President McKinley, while he was still a senator passed the first tariff that included reciprocity, which in international trade, involves the adjustment of one nation's tariff rates in exchange for similar adjustments or concessions from another nation, which is fair. But, it was actually President Benjamin Harrison that persuaded Republicans to support provisions for reciprocity that were added to Senator McKinley's tariff.

However, the average rate of the tariff was 48% and so high that exporters couldn't get their products into foreign markets that retaliated against the high tariff. Many of the supporters of the Tariff of 1890 were drummed out of office in the election of 1892.

There's no good thing that can't be abused, including free trade, protectionism, and ice cream.

The economic policies of Alexander Hamilton and

Henry Clay were successful for 124 years. The Federal Reserve and free trade turned five and dime stores into dollar stores—not the economic policies of the 19th century.

How's that comparative advantage working for us now? Americans had abundant national wealth, and potential wealth, thanks to the self-sufficiency we enjoyed due to America's large area geographically, the diverse skills of our human resources and our abundant natural resources. Free trade within the United States; protection of our economic borders and the resultant mutually beneficial exchange through competition made America the greatest nation on earth from the 19th century through much of the 20th century. Constitutional tariffs and the economic policies of Alexander Hamilton and Henry Clay made us so successful as a nation, that even after free trade was introduced into our economy, we were able to coast for decades without realizing that we were slowing down, despite The Great Depression and its destruction wrought by the speculative practices of the Federal Reserve—you're right, that's not true. It's an insult to the generation that lived through The Great Depression to say that there were decades of coasting after free trade and the Federal Reserve. It actually took 16 years from the time of the Federal Reserve, free trade and the installation of federal income and payroll taxes that pay for the free trade program, to bring America to its knees. It wasn't until after WWII that we were able to form the appearance of a recovery from that debacle. America was not yet threatened industrially because our main rivals had been decimated by two world wars, so we grew, and survived multiple attacks, until our manufacturers became commodities, to be bought and sold like corn, wheat, and pork bellies.

How did free trade work prior to the Civil War? It didn't work at all in the North. Free trade was rejected in the North in favor of the American System. Domestic industry was protected from foreign predators and America's industrial revolution made Britain's look like they were in reverse. The South on the other hand, embraced free trade and Adam Smith's math that a slave was worth twice his maintenance, but a free man would cost you double, because of his wife and their four children. The computed rule was that a free man had to raise four children, because two of them would die before reaching maturity. Six people were expected to live off the maintenance it would take to keep two alive, until two of them statistically died, and then four would live off the maintenance for two. The minimum was required, according to their study; else the race of laborers would not survive past the first generation. Slaves simplified the math for plantation owners, so they went with Adam Smith's first recommendation for their workforce which was, that a slave was worth double what it cost to keep him.

Free trade advocates don't place blame for America's plight on free trade but instead blame Americans for their own unemployment. Just as this isn't true— mostly, neither is this an indictment of Southerners and their heritage, nor necessarily on plantation owners who were for that time, the one-percent. This, like today in modern America is how a mere splinter of the one-percent were able to hold not only their own people hostage to unemployment through reprehensible policies like keeping humans as property, but were able to bluff and bully an entire nation. Southerners in the ninety-nine percent class aren't great because of the South's slave history; they were great in *spite* of it. Millions migrated north where landless free men could find employment, but millions stayed behind despite their inability to compete as laborers against the wages of a slave labor workforce.

Resentment today is expressed toward the Hispanic population for allegedly stealing our jobs through low wage labor. Is it inconceivable that landless free people of the 19th century South had resentment for the victims of slavery who they couldn't hope to compete with on wages? Southerners were fully aware that the Civil War was a rich man's war and a poor man's fight.

It was constitutionally illegal to levy tariffs on other states. The South fought vigorously for free trade with Britain, but refused to trade with northern industries whom they had the advantage of constitutionally mandated free trade with. The South went as far as to levy tariffs against Kentucky as punishment for Kentucky's support of the American System of economics. Senator Henry Clay gave an anecdote from South Carolina Representative, Eldred Simkins, who previously supported the Carolina measures:

"The honorable gentleman from South Carolina says that a profitable trade was carried on from the West, through the Saluda gap, in mules, horses, and other livestock, which has been checked by the operation of the tariff. It is true that such a trade was carried on between Kentucky and South Carolina, mutually beneficial to both parties; but, several years ago, resolutions, at popular meetings, in Carolina, were adopted, not to purchase the produce of Kentucky, by way of punishment for her attachment to the tariff. They must have supposed us as stupid as the sires of one of the descriptions of the stock of which that trade consisted, if they imagined that their resolutions would affect our principles. Our drovers cracked their whips, blew their horns, and passed the Saluda gap, to other markets, where better humors existed, and equal or greater profits were made. I have heard of your successor in the House of Representatives, Mr. President, this anecdote; That he

joined in the adoption of those resolutions, but when, about Christmas, he applied to one of his South Carolina neighbors to purchase the regular supply of pork for the ensuing year, he found that he had to give two prices for it; and he declared if that were the patriotism on which the resolutions were based, he would not conform to them, and, in point of fact, laid in his annual stock of pork by purchase from the first passing Kentucky drover. That trade, now partially resumed, was maintained by the sale of the western productions on the one side, and Carolina money on the other. From that condition of it, the gentleman from South Carolina might have drawn this conclusion, that an advantageous trade may exist, although one of the parties it pays in specie for the productions which he purchases from the other; and, consequently, that it does now follow, if we did not purchase British fabrics, that it might not be the interest of England to purchase our raw material of cotton. The Kentucky drover received the South Carolina specie, or, taking bills, or evidences of deposit in the banks, carried these home, and disposing of them to the merchant, he brought out goods, of foreign or domestic manufacture, in return. Such is the circuitous nature of trade and remittance, which no nation understands better than Great Britain." (2)

Further explanation of Henry Clay's speech is seldom warranted, but this is what he was saying in more contemporary language. The honorable gentleman from South Carolina that Kentucky Senator, Henry

Clay referred to was Senator Robert Y. Hayne of South Carolina, and his assertion that prior to the tariff, South Carolina had enjoyed a profitable trade from Kentucky through the Saluda Gap, which was a trail that lead from the North Carolina mountains to the South Carolina flat country. Senator Clay verified Senator Hayne's claim that mutually beneficial trade had indeed been carried on between Kentucky and South Carolina, but that several years previous, Carolina had adopted resolutions to not purchase products from Kentucky as punishment for Kentucky's support of the tariffs. Senator Clay said that the Carolinians must have thought Kentuckians as stupid as mules if they thought their resolutions would make Kentucky compromise its principles. Their drovers (cattle drivers or teamsters) passed the Saluda gap and went on to other markets where their business was welcome and customers had a better temperament.

He then went on to relate an anecdote from Representative Eldred Simkins of South Carolina, who endorsed the resolutions to punish Kentucky for supporting the tariffs, but when Christmas came and he placed his annual order to a local farmer for pork, the price was double to buy from the South Carolina farmer. Mr. Simkins said that if that was what counted for patriotism in South Carolina, he would have no part of it, and placed his annual order for pork with the first passing Kentucky drover that came through. Trade was partially resumed by the trade of pork from Kentucky in the west, in exchange for currency from South Carolina. Mr. Clay went on to say that South Carolina might do well to assume that advantageous trade would still exist with Great Britain if we don't *buy* their fabrics, but instead sell them our raw cotton material in exchange for currency. He said that this was the nature of the circle of trade and payment, which no nation understood better than Great Britain.

Free trade is the tool that Britain used in its attempt to keep this nation dependent on them for manufactured goods, and it was an effective tool. It was men like Alexander Hamilton and Henry Clay that refused to buy the rope that was meant to bind us. The American System worked for no less than 124 years. Free trade has seldom been to our domestic benefit, but it could be, if it was fair and equal. Henry Clay deferred to one of the Lords of British Parliament of that time to speak of Britain's weapon of choice. Lord Goderich said, "It was idle for us to endeavor to persuade other nations to join with us in adopting the principles of what was called 'free trade.' Other nations knew, as well as the noble lord opposite, and those who acted with him, what we meant by 'free trade', was nothing more nor less than, by means of the great advantages we enjoyed, to get a monopoly of all their markets for our manufactures, and to prevent them, one and all, from ever becoming manufacturing nations." (3)

To be "idle", means to waste time. Lord Goderich apparently had more confidence than was merited of our intelligence and common sense necessary for self-preservation. He supposed it a waste of time for Britain to trick America into adopting the principles of free trade, for he reckoned we would never fall for it—but we did.

The horror of it is that Washington even screwed that up. The purpose of the British System was to take advantage of less developed nations for their raw materials while maintaining their manufacturing base in Britain.

I think we misread the directions, or maybe Britain is still mad at us for selling them the watered down version of the P-38 Lightning and gave us the wrong directions on purpose.

***

In Defense of The American System

Chapter 3 Free Trade Slavery

One of the constants that can be counted on in life is problem solving via the process of elimination. Whether you're the progeny of Albert Einstein or a simpleton, it's reliable. Belief systems have been challenged and changed many times with this valuable tool. The process of elimination is the process of deleting incorrect options until the possibility of the remaining option being correct is close to 100%.

Occam's razor is another favorite and works well in conjunction with the process of elimination. The razor states that one should proceed to simpler theories until simplicity can be traded for greater explanatory power, though a simpler definition would be, "When I hear the drumming of hooves, I don't think unicorns, I think horses.", assuming that is, you don't live in North Korea that claims to have unicorns.

Speaking of North Korea, they have taken Free Trade and outsourcing to the next level. There's no need to ship your factory to North Korea to employ forced labor slaves. North Korea is now outsourcing its workers to other countries.

North Korea ships workers to Siberia to log timber that is in turn sold to Great Britain. The good workers are kept in wretched conditions and work ten years in Siberian timber, with visits home every three to five years. North Korean workers that are not deemed productive are sent home (or somewhere) at the end of three years. (1)

Free trade has *always* been rooted in slavery. Its motivation for implementation has been in place from the founding of our nation and cotton exports to the most common items you buy at Wal-Mart.

Occasionally, a public figure associated with a product line that is manufactured in a foreign country, whose workers die in a factory fire because all the exits are locked; in order to better manage their slave or dirt wage workforce; garners attention from the media. The public figure, sometimes a celebrity, feigns horror and ignorance at the wretchedness of the safety and working conditions associated with the factory of death for the product line bearing their name. They make a scripted promise to investigate and fix the problem and soon the story dies of loneliness.

Bangladesh has about 4,500 garment factories and is the world's biggest exporter of clothing after China. These workers are not forced labor slaves. Their minimum wage is 18 cents per hour which, according to the World Bank is comparable to a U.S. laborer working for 55 cents per hour. At least 300 people have died in Bangladesh garment factories from 2006 to 2012. At the 2012 factory fire in Dhaka, Bangladesh, where 112 workers died, at least three American companies, Walmart, Disney, and Sears, whose clothing was made at the factory, have denied knowledge that their garments were made there, and claim that the clothing was made there without their permission. Workers who survived the fire said that the emergency exits were locked. The owner of the factory claimed no one told him that he was supposed to have an emergency exit accessible from the outside. (2)

The founding father of free trade slavery, Adam Smith first published his bible of free trade in 1776, and it is still to this day studiously worshipped by students of economics. Slaves are considered an ideal workforce because a slave is computed to be worth twice his maintenance. In the absence of slaves, Adam Smith grudgingly concedes that an able bodied worker's wages must at least be sufficient to maintain him, and, on occasion, be somewhat more—because otherwise it would be impossible for him to bring up a family, and the race of such workmen would not survive past the first generation. (3)

He does not endorse the opinion of Irish-French economist, Richard Cantillon, but he does say that Mr. Cantillon seems to suppose that workers must make double their maintenance, which includes the minimum required for the maintenance of the worker, and the other share for a wife and four children. Cantillon based this on a family of four and not six because the worker would have to father four children, of whom two would die before reaching maturity, based on mortality rates. Adam Smith benevolently, if not skeptically, conceded that paying a free man the lowest that is required for his existence is consistent with common humanity—thank you ever so much for that kindness Mr. Smith. (4)

There is opportunity under the Free Trade model to improve your situation and earn more than the minimum required to keep you alive. In a thriving economy where there is a shortage of workers, employers must bid against each other to compete for available workers, and by necessity, wages will increase. This competition can only occur in an economy that is thriving and has a shortage of workers. It isn't applicable to a static economy, and wages go down in a stagnant economy. (5) But there is no shortage of slaves in third world countries. Slaves were expensive in the pre-Civil War South, but today you can buy two grown men for as little as $80.

This is the 21st century. We can't live under the 18th and 19th century ideals of opponents to free trade like the Federalists, Whigs and the early Republicans, but neither can Adam Smith's model for a slave workforce be viable today—right?

The computer you are using serves double duty as a functional monument to the ideals of free trade, Adam Smith, and basic economic theory that is taught in colleges and universities today. Computer makers would not want you to know the advantages that free trade has given them in the United States and globally. They have an unassailable advantage, thanks to their business model in Asian countries where parts are produced and shipped to the United States. The advantage that computer companies enjoy over domestic production in the United States is the advantage of human trafficking. Human hunters that prey on the desperation of job seekers in poor countries like Indonesia, Bangladesh, Cambodia and the Philippines, present themselves as a placement service for computer manufacturers. Job seekers, who are able, scrounge up by whatever means, the thousands of dollars required by the "brokers" for the job seeker's "placement fees". The broker promises the job seekers ten times what they will actually receive. The workers are forced to sign multi-year contracts and surrender their passports, so that if they try to run away, they are subject to arrest, imprisonment and caning (beaten with a long stick) before being expelled from the country. The workers are in fact paid. If they never spend a penny on themselves after company deductions for room, board and taxes, they may be able to save $500 over a three year period.

When politicians from countries like Malaysia, whose computer manufacturers are willful participants in human trafficking are confronted with these allegations, they categorically deny that such practices take place in their country, and that the allegations are false. (5)

The American public is somewhat aware of human trafficking worldwide regarding forced prostitution, because it sells well in media like the movie industry. What the American public is less likely to be aware of is human trafficking worldwide in the form of forced labor slavery. Slavery and the importation of slave made products is outlawed in America and yet we reap the benefits of a slave based economy every day via the global supply chain. In 2005, the United Nations' International Labour Organization said that forced labor was a global problem affecting almost all countries of the world, claiming at least 12.3 million men, women and children. Most of the victims of this slave trade are from Africa, Asia and Latin America. The ILO optimistically forecast that with help, forced labor slavery could be eradicated by the year 2015. The reality is that by 2012, victims of forced labor slavery, who are the backbone that support the global supply chain for American imports has risen to over 20 million, and by some estimates is already at 27 million, which would conservatively place the number by 2015 at 25 million forced labor slaves. (6)

The number of forced prostitution slaves worldwide is about 2 million. The conservative number of forced labor slaves worldwide is 20.9 million. Does anyone think that U.S. multi-national corporations whose entire business model is based on free trade, would just passively hope that statistics like these would never come to light? We buy forced labor slave produced products that we use every day in our homes and life. In my book, "Battered Nation Syndrome", I explained how U.S. multinational corporations and politicians work together to heap accolades on the American worker for being the most productive workers in the world, while simultaneously blaming those same workers for working too hard and producing too much to make room for other job seekers, thereby stifling job growth. (7)

These same U.S. multinational corporations are begging for U.S. tax breaks under the guise of job creation, but refusing to disclose how many of those jobs are created overseas. The government is complicit by requiring these corporations to report their overseas hiring data to the Commerce Department, but promising not to disclose these figures to the general public.

The purpose of this is almost unknown, but relatively easy to explain, and nothing short of diabolical. The U.S. government helps corporations hide these figures because it helps perpetuate the false narrative of lauding American workers as being the most productive workers in the world, and simultaneously blaming their productivity for stifling job growth. Compound that deception with the latest narrative, that since American productivity is stifling job creation, we, the people, should accept our current economic woe as the "New Normal".

The purpose of our government collaborating with corporations to hide their overseas hiring figures is relatively easy to understand and also explains the myth of American productivity. As America's debt burden continues to pile on in the guise of stimulus, American workers are patronized by Republicans, Democrats and Libertarians alike with accolades for being the most productive workers in the world. The claim of American productivity is in the kindest terms, a myth.

Americans can out produce any labor force on the planet. That's not bravado; that's history. That fact is being exploited by bad people who lie to us about our current Herculean productivity levels by giving ten workers credit for the work of a hundred.

You want to believe people when they're telling you how great you are, but the truth is we're not that great. We're actually not very good at all in respect to productivity—compared to what we're credited for, but on paper we look great. Media outlets looking to exploit our opinion of ourselves are fanning phony outrage by telling the few people who do have jobs that they're responsible for the nation's unemployment rate because their increased productivity is stifling job growth.

The myth of American productivity is refuted by exposing the difference between "Domestic Productivity" and "Supply Chain Productivity", or more accurately, "Global Supply Chain Productivity". The myth is perpetuated because both are counted as "American Productivity". They are far from the same thing. Domestic productivity means you have a job. Global supply chain productivity means someone in another country has a job, and, if they're not working as a forced labor slave, they have a paycheck too. The American worker gets the credit for being so productive and the blame for being too productive to make room for anyone else in the workforce. It's diabolical. The most insulting excuse I've heard yet for our poor economy is that Americans are so productive that we should accept high unemployment rates because we're producing so much with so few people.

I've seen the tired old refrain reported on both CNN and FOX that if we punish companies who have moved overseas that it will backfire and kill American productivity. Please let me explain what they don't want you to know about their *technically* correct claim. American productivity should be just that— American, but corporations that have moved their factories overseas so they could sell us the products we used to make, still get credit for Chinese made goods that count as American productivity. In fact, Chinese made goods have astronomically increased American productivity and here's a simple example to explain how.

1: An imaginary American company has a factory in Huntington, WV making brake rotors with 100 employees. They make 1000 brake rotors a day.

2: Another imaginary American company across the street with only ten employees also makes 1000 brake rotors a day but their rotors come from a factory in China. The Chinese factory ships the rotors to the company where they are packaged for sale in the U.S. Because the rotors are packaged in the U.S., the number of workers per rotor built is counted as American productivity. The U.S. government collaborates with these corporations and credits the company with only ten employees as having a productivity level ten times higher than their competitor across the street that makes brake rotors in America. (8)

What is good for free trade as we know it is not good for Domestic Productivity. What is good for free trade is great for Global Supply Chain Productivity. Domestic Productivity means you have a job making televisions. Supply Chain Productivity means someone in another country has a job making televisions, but it's ok. It's so cheap you can probably afford it with your downsized paycheck from your job working in a service industry, and best of all, that foreign made television might count as overall American Productivity. With the money you save, you can buy a t-shirt made by forced labor Bangladeshi orphan slaves with the free trade slogan, "American workers are the most productive workers in the world!"

***

In Defense of The American System

Chapter 4 Free Trade Morality

Using Commerce Department statistics for the years from 2000 to 2009, foreign jobs added by U.S. Corporations increased to almost 2 million while domestic layoffs reached 4 million. Our workforce is moving overseas due to the hiring practices of U.S. multinational corporations. There is only passive lip service given to the plight of American workers. Americans are patronized as they're told that the jobs bleeding from our borders are jobs we don't want anyway because they're going to be replaced with better jobs. Meanwhile, multi-national corporations are lobbying for more tax breaks for job creation but refuse to say where those jobs will be located. (1)

American manufacturing jobs disappear as displaced workers are forced into service industry jobs and then told that it's an upgrade. Americans want to build things they can look at, point to and tell their children, "I made that." Americans would rather build things than service or sell products whose names they cannot pronounce from countries they can't find on a map.

Recent presidential polls for the 2016 presidential election show that Americans are not duped regarding Wall Street's record profits during the same time that unemployment went up 100%. Neither American nor domestic productivity are driving the profits on Wall Street; supply chain productivity is driving the profits. The U.S. government and multinational corporations that used to operate in America and now operate overseas, intentionally hide the breakdown of their domestic and overseas employment numbers. Their shell game is reinforced by talking mannequins in both political parties and pundits who praise American productivity which is pure fantasy.

Supply chain productivity is being lumped in with domestic productivity which is then sold as American productivity. Americans no longer believe our government on how to grow the economy when they've repeatedly outsourced our jobs.

How many people actually buy the reasoning that the jobs we're losing are jobs we don't want? Talk to almost anyone in the service industry who lost their job in manufacturing to a dirt wage or forced slave laborer overseas and ask them what they think when they walk into Wal-Mart. Do they look at the poorly made cheap products they can buy and think, "Boy, I sure don't miss making clothes, shoes, batteries, tools, televisions, lawn mowers, textiles or appliances anymore." I doubt they thank the titans of government and corporations for mass imports because they can buy cheap tchotchkes with their shrinking paycheck.

A poor nation is created when its manufacturing

industry is forfeited and replaced with service industries. The overwhelming majority of Americans don't want our manufacturing shipped overseas, but the brain trusts of their political parties do, and they cater to the fabricated hot button issues of their base while playing a shell game of distraction to achieve their goal of globalization and profits through forced slave labor. China is only too willing to be their facilitator.

Many have said at one time, or many times, "I don't care how you get it done. Just do it." Bad people use that logic too.

The Republican Party doesn't care how many guns you own or how many times you go to church as long as you support international free trade agreements.

The Democrat Party doesn't care how much you demonize big corporations or how many babies you abort as long as you support international free trade agreements.

The Libertarian Party doesn't care how much pot you smoke or how many government agencies you dismantle as long as you support international free trade agreements.

The little known Constitution Party according to Article I, Section 8 of the U.S. Constitution advocates a return to the example set by the American System and the elimination of Federal income, payroll, and estate taxes and a return to a system similar to that which was in place for most of our nation's history by supporting the tariff based revenue system that our founding fathers put in place, specifically, Alexander Hamilton. The U.S. tariff on any foreign import would not be less than the difference between the foreign item's cost of production and the cost of production of a similar item produced in the United States, including the cost of compensation, fringe benefits and the environmental cost of doing business according to federal, state, and local governments.

I closely watched the Constitution Party during the 2012 election season. They had an economic plan that we see resonating with millions of Americans during the 2016 election season. What did the Constitution Party do with the strongest plank in their platform— nothing. They paraded around the country with a giant paper mache Obama head that blew smoke rings, and seldom if ever got on message about their economic policy.

The string pullers through international free trade agreements have orchestrated the destruction of American industry at the rate of more than 15 plant closings per day from 2001 to 2010 and more than 23 plant closings per day in 2010 alone, all in the name of Mom, apple pie and free trade.

The people responsible for closing those plants and their sycophants say, "Get an education and you'll never miss those factory jobs. Those were jobs

Americans don't want anyway." Someone I respect mused that one engineer can design enough product to keep 3,000 laborers busy, but I'd like to reduce that figure by 90% for the benefit of free trade advocates. If one engineer can design enough product for 300 laborers, how long will it take before former laborers with spanking new engineering diplomas find themselves bereft of job opportunities? If the average IQ in China is four points higher than the average IQ in the United States, do they need our engineers? Does anyone in America doubt that China will copy our designs, steal our technology and sell our own fat rumps back to us in the form of products we used to make and use in the course of our everyday lives with unpronounceable Chinese brand names? Americans can make more money per hour collecting aluminum cans from the side of the road than China's paid laborers. These low paid laborers aren't counted among the 27 million forced slave laborers that stock many of the products on our store shelves. Chinese prison laborers produce virtually every Christmas decoration that use to adorn our homes.

The town where I live puts up decorations every year between November and January. The banners say "Happy Holidays". A lady came running out of her house that was covered with Christmas decorations made by Chinese prison labor and demanded the banner be taken down from the pole in front of her house because it said "Happy Holidays" instead of "Merry Christmas". If only we knew how we mock and indict ourselves.

One need look no further than the arguments of free trade advocates to see the evidence against free trade. While defending their position on free trade, they invariably bring up why it's bad. Before defending their position they expose the unpopular negatives before assuring you that it doesn't apply to the United States. It can go something like this:

"It is not unusual to hear the following reservations expressed about free trade: 'Free trade harms large segments of U.S. workers.' 'Free trade degrades the environment.' 'Free trade exploits poor countries.' 'Free trade cheapens our dollar.' We have all heard these criticisms and lots of others. But free trade is good for consumers because products are cheaper for the consumer"

If you're a parent, then you must already be acquainted with this strategy from your children. Children—and adults, employ this preemptive tactic of bringing up valid objections, before assuring you that their awareness of the pitfalls demonstrates exactly why it won't happen to them. Then they hard sell you on *all* the reasons why buying magic beans is a good idea.

Senator Henry Clay, in February, 1832, debated the immorality of free trade on the floor of the Senate.

Free trade advocates had invoked the names of prominent Englishmen who favored America opening its borders to free trade with Great Britain. Mr. Clay expressed his disdain of resorting to the authority of foreign powers to set policy for what was best for America. He said:

"I dislike this resort to authority, and especially *foreign* and *interested* authority, for the support of principles of public policy. I would greatly prefer to meet gentlemen upon the broad ground of fact, of experience, and of reason; but, since they will appeal to British names and authority, I feel myself compelled to imitate their bad example. Allow me to quote from the speech of a member of the British Parliament."

"It was idle for us to endeavor to persuade other nations to join with us in adopting the principles of what was called 'free trade.' Other nations knew, as well as the noble lord opposite, and those who acted with him, what we meant by 'free trade', was nothing more nor less than, by means of the great advantages we enjoyed, to get a monopoly of all their markets for our manufactures, and to prevent them, one and all, from ever becoming manufacturing nations."

"When the system of reciprocity and free trade had been proposed to a French ambassador, his remark was, that the plan was excellent in theory, but, to make it fair in practice, it would be necessary to defer the attempt to put it in execution for half a century, until France should be on the same footing with Great Britain, in marine, in manufactures, in capital, and the many other peculiar advantages which it now enjoyed. The policy that France acted on, was that of encouraging its native manufactures, and it was a wise policy; because, if it were freely to admit our manufactures, it would speedily be reduced to the rank of an agricultural nation; and therefore a poor nation, as all must be that depend exclusively upon agriculture. America acted, too, upon the same principle with France. America legislated for futurity—legislated for an increasing population. America, too, was prosperous under this system. In twenty years, America would be independent of England for manufactures altogether..."

"But since the peace, France, Germany, America, and all the other countries of the world, had proceeded upon the principle of encouraging and protecting native manufactures."

During that speech in the Senate, in February, 1832, Henry Clay spoke about the amendment to the Tariff of 1824, which was the Tariff of 1828, otherwise known as "The Tariff of Abominations."

"An amendment of the system was proposed in 1828, to the history of which I refer with no agreeable recollections. The bill of that year, in some of its provisions, was framed on principles directly adverse to the declared wishes of the friends of the policy of protection. I have heard (without

vouching for the fact) that it was so framed, upon the advice of a prominent citizen, now abroad, with the view of ultimately defeating the bill, and with assurances that, being altogether unacceptable to the friends of the American System, the bill would be lost. Be that as it may, the most exceptionable features of the bill were stamped upon it, against the earnest remonstrances of the friends of the system, by the votes of southern members, upon a principle, I think, as unsound in legislation as it is reprehensible in ethics. The bill was passed, notwithstanding, it having been deemed better to take the bad along with the good which it contained, than reject it altogether. Subsequent legislation has corrected very much the error then perpetrated, but still that measure is vehemently denounced by gentlemen who contributed to make it what is was."

To those present during Henry Clay's speech, there was nothing cryptic about his disgust for the amendment to the Tariff of 1824 that was proposed in 1828, also known as, "The Tariff of Abominations". What was the reprehensible act he alluded to? Obviously those in the chamber knew what he was talking about. John C. Calhoun, one of the chief architects of the Tariff of 1828 laid out in an 1837 speech, the strategy behind the bill that prompted Henry Clay to label the ethics of it as reprehensible. The truth of the matter is that the critics of the tariff were actually its authors. Opponents of protectionism and the American System collaborated in a conspiracy to defeat the Tariff of 1824 and pave the way for free trade. Their plan backfired in spectacular fashion.

The Tariff of 1828 was part of a series of tariffs that began after the War of 1812 and the Napoleonic Wars. Tariffs had been lowered as American industry became more competitive against Great Britain and the rest of Europe, but the blockade of Europe led British manufacturers to offer goods in America at low prices that American manufacturers often could not match. The first of this series of protective tariffs was passed by Congress in 1816, increasing the average cost of tariffs from 6.5% to 20.2%. The tariff rates were increased again in 1824 to an average of 22.3%. Southern states and particularly South Carolina contended that the tariff was unconstitutional and were opposed to anything less than free and open trade, but Western agricultural states favored the protection tariffs, as well as manufacturers in New England.

In an elaborate scheme—conspiracy—to prevent passage of still higher tariffs, while at the same time appealing to Andrew Jackson's supporters in the North, Vice President, John C. Calhoun and other southerners crafted a tariff bill that would make materials imported by the New England states prohibitively expensive. It was believed that

President John Quincy Adam's supporters in New England, the National Republicans or as they would later be called, Whigs, would uniformly oppose the bill for this reason and that the southern legislators could then withdraw their support, killing the legislation while blaming it on New England. Henry Clay labeled the ethics behind the legislation as reprehensible. The Tariff of 1828 would raise protective tariffs from an average of 22.3% to 35%.

Vice President John C. Calhoun admitted the plan of conspiracy in a speech he gave in 1837 when he recounted the events of 1828 and defended the actions taken by himself and his fellow Southern members. A high-tariff bill was to be put before the House. It was to contain not only a high general range of duties, but duties especially high on the raw materials which New England wanted the duties to be low. It would satisfy the protective demands of the Western and Middle States, but at the same time, be obnoxious to the New England members. All of the Jackson men, the protectionists from the North and the free-traders from the South, would unite to prevent any amendments; that bill, and no other, was to be voted on. When the final vote came, the southern men were to turn around and vote against their own measure. The New England men and the Adams men in general, would be unable to accept the measure, and would also vote against it. Combined, they would prevent its passage, even though the Jackson men from the North voted for it. The result expected was that no tariff bill at all would be passed during the session, which was the object of the southern wing of the opposition. On the other hand, the blame for defeating American protection would be cast on the Adams party, which was the object of the Jacksonians of the North. The tariff bill would be defeated, and yet the Jackson men would be able to parade as the true "friends" of the people. (2)

The Democrat Party had miscalculated. Despite the insertion of import duties by Democrats, calculated to be unacceptable to New England industries, specifically on raw wool imports essential to the wool textile industry, the New Englanders failed to defeat the legislation, and their plan backfired. (3)

John C. Calhoun was Vice President to John Quincy Adams. If his actions were not treasonous, they were most assuredly traitorous to his president. The net result of Calhoun's conspiracy was the defeat of President Adams in the following election. Calhoun then became Vice President to the victor, Andrew Jackson. Calhoun vigorously opposed the tariff that he was the architect of, even going so far as anonymously authoring a pamphlet in December, 1828 in which he urged for the nullification of the tariff in South Carolina. An open split occurred between President Jackson and Vice President

Calhoun. Calhoun finally resigned on December 10, 1832, after President Jackson refused to lower the tariff enough to the satisfaction of Calhoun and the South Carolina Democrats with the Tariff of 1832.

During Senator Clay's speech in February, 1832, he rightly pointed out the morality of keeping in place the proven record and system of protectionism, that if overturned, would result in the destruction of domestic industry and the public faith from the thousands upon thousands who had depended on and invested in a system of protection that was assumed to be a settled issue, dating as far back as 1789, and funding as much as 97.9% of the nation's budget without need for income or payroll tax upon the people:

"Thus, sir, has this great system of protection been gradually built, stone upon stone, and step by step, from the 4th of July, 1789, down to the present period. In every stage of its progress it has received the deliberate sanction of Congress. A vast majority of the people of the United States has approved, and continues to approve it. Every chief magistrate of the United States, from Washington to the present, in some form or other, has given to it the authority of his name; and, however the opinions of the existing president are interpreted south of Mason and Dixon's line, on the north they are, at least, understood to favor the establishment of a judicious tariff."

"The question, therefore, which we are now called upon to

determine, is not whether we shall establish a new and doubtful system of policy, just proposed, and for the first time presented to our consideration; but whether we shall break down and destroy a long established system, patiently and carefully built up, and sanctioned, during a series of years, again and again, by the nation and its highest and most revered authorities. And are we not bound deliberately to consider whether we can proceed to this work of destruction without a violation of the public faith? The people of the United States have justly supposed that the policy of protecting their industry, against foreign legislation and foreign industry, was fully settled, not by a single act, but by repeated and deliberate acts of government, performed at distant and frequent intervals. In full confidence that the policy was firmly and unchangeably fixed, thousands upon thousands have invested their capital, purchased a vast amount of real and other estate, made permanent establishments, and accommodated their industry. Can we expose to utter and irretrievable ruin this countless multitude, without justly incurring the reproach of violating the national faith?"

The Trans Pacific Partnership agreement includes the U.S., Australia, Singapore, Chile, Peru, Brunei, New Zealand, Malaysia and Viet Nam. If the TPP delivers on the promise of removing the tariffs on U.S. exports to those countries, it should go a long way toward helping our situation with trade imbalance. If it doesn't deliver on the promises of politicians, then it will likely be more exportation of U.S. manufacturing jobs abroad, and give our factories in China a low wage alternative to the rising cost of Chinese manufacturing. Hopefully TPP is not a scheme to move manufacturing jobs abroad where cheaper labor can be found after current cheap labor rates rise to an unacceptable level. China is fast approaching a labor rate of $2 an hour.

You can follow the advice of the current Republicans, who were once the guardians of domestic prosperity through protection of American industry. We can follow the advice of the Libertarians and eliminate the Environmental Protection Agency, the Food and Drug Administration, OSHA, the Federal Trade Commission, the National Labor Relations Board, FBI, Social Security, Welfare, Minimum Wage and Public Schools. That might fix our competitiveness. Americans might finally be able to compete with the wages of forced slave laborers overseas. If Americans truly want to accommodate the Libertarians, we should take the lines off the highways too. No one should be told what side of the road they have to drive on. We can take the advice of the Democrats and embrace free trade while pretending to care about the environment when one need only look at the pollution in China to know that bringing industry back to America and our environmental policies would do more to cut pollution than any other proposal the U.S. government will ever put forth while they pretend to care about the expediency of working on the climate change they believe is more dangerous than terrorism.

The American System isn't a theory; it's not a new and improved gift wrapped version of the old failed promises of free trade. The American System has a proven and well documented track record of improving the lives of all Americans; not just the 99% and not just the 1%, but all Americans.

The American System protects American jobs, it protects domestic producing corporations, and it protects Americans from an ethically weak sociopathic government looking for handouts from multinational corporate lobbyists. China's markets and the American corporations that fled there are collapsing because they glutted themselves on cheap labor, equipment and production in favor of high profits that are unsustainable due to the exportation of the jobs needed by consumers to keep those corporations in business. The large department stores had their boom days, but as America got poorer, Walmart boomed, and as America grows poorer still, Walmart wains as thrift stores thrive. The free trade system has saved America so much money, we're broke. Politicians and the news media will never quit pretending they don't know why China's stock market is collapsing. It's all tied to their manufacturing... which used to be our manufacturing. China has taken our jobs and hence our ability to buy their junk so now they have piles of junk and Americans are left with service industry jobs and government assistance.

Trade with other nations has historically increased during times of protective tariffs. Domestic establishment and protection of U.S. manufacturers increases the creation of wealth for American consumers, and this gives new powers of consumption, which result in the purchase of foreign as well as domestic products. A poor nation can never be a great consuming nation. Its poverty will limit its consumption to bare subsistence when its manufacturing industry is forfeited and replaced with service industries and agrarianism. The family farm and gardening are coming back, and though, to some extent can be credited to nostalgia or environmental concerns; more people are growing their own food out of necessity and not as a hobby.

Free trade's effects upon the wage earning capabilities of U.S. citizens has been catastrophic. Minimum wage is meant to be a mandated hourly wage for entry level employees and least able members of the workforce. The minimum wage remained unchanged for 10 years from 1997 to 2007. In 2009 the rate was increased to $7.25, but as of 2013, it was proposed to be raised to $9.00 per hour. The fact that market forces including supply and demand are important factors considered when setting minimum wage rates means the proposition of raising the new minimum to as high as $15.00 doesn't bode well for the government's confidence in our domestic economic future.

If morality can be divorced from slavery, but not from self-preservation, are the effects of slavery negated while supporting free trade? Free trade degrades labor. Free trade exploits poor countries. Free trade retards economic growth.

Replace "free trade" with "slavery" and the criticism is the same. Just as surely as morality cannot be divorced from slavery, neither can it be divorced from free trade. Free trade as it's been for hundreds of years is inseparable from slavery. Free trade thus far has never existed global scale. Trade implies at least two parties. To be free, it should be fair, equal, and reciprocal. By throwing our ports open to the admission of foreign goods, free of all duty, what ports of any other foreign nation do we have free admission of our surplus produce?

***

Chapter 5 Impetus of War

Most historians agree that slavery was the impetus of the American Civil War. Secession romanticists prefer to blame protectionist tariffs as the reason for the South's secession. They do concede that while slavery was an unfortunate occurrence, it was not the reason why the South seceded, but that Northern opposition to free trade was.

In homage to Henry Clay, let me say, I give way with pleasure to these explanations, which I hope will always be made when debating the cause of the civil war.

One of the South's major objections to tariffs was their claim that they paid about 75% of all federal taxes. In 1860, tariffs on imported goods accounted for 95% of the income for the federal government. The unavoidable question is, if the South paid 75% of all federal taxes, and import tariffs accounted for 95% of the federal government's income, then the South was buying a lot of imports. Southern plantation owners were not content to buy American products because they felt no status attached to those goods, while luxury imports from Britain, whether of higher quality or not, were more exotic. The South paid high federal taxes through the tariff system because they had no desire to do business with northern manufacturers, but did feel compelled to buy their goods from the British as reciprocity for their cotton exports to Europe instead of trading their goods for currency. They were essentially operating on the barter system with their foreign partners and then paying the tax on the bartered goods they received in return for their cotton exports.

The Free Trade, every state for themselves mentality contributed to the defeat of the South during the Civil War. The South was populated with anti-Federalists who believed in very limited government and state's sovereignty above all. The Democrat Party started out as the anti-Federalists that opposed economic protectionism and the fiscal policies of the Federalists and Alexander Hamilton. They supported slavery and free trade with Great Britain and Europe. The anti-Federalists supported a confederation of states instead of a union, which would have been essentially the same as Europe, with each state being as sovereign as a nation with virtually no authority or control from a central government. If America were still under the Articles of Confederation instead of a federal government, subject to the Constitution, calling a Virginian an American would bear no more weight or meaning than calling a German a European. Under the Articles of Confederation, Americans would be classified as Americans by scant more than geography. Each state would be responsible for minting its own currency and fielding its own military, which would have made smaller poorer nation states easy prey for less than neighborly states. Considering all the wars that have taken place over the centuries between European states, it's baffling that this option was ever considered viable. The anti-Federalists eventually became The Democratic-Republican Party, who became the Democrat Party.

By the time of the Civil War, the North had a vast railroad system with new lines constantly being added. In the South, bickering between the states prevented the construction of interstate railroad systems.

In the North, any train could be transported to any part of the Union railroad system and placed on any track. In the South, there was no standardized track gauge, meaning that a train that could run on one track line, could not operate on another.

The South's main interest economically was an agrarian society of farmers and planters with very little industrialization. Free white men, who weren't land owners or were unskilled, had virtually no place in the economic system of slavery because they could never hope to compete on wages with the labor of slaves.

The utopia that the South was perceived to be before the Civil War quickly exposed its flaws when war broke out. There were few foundries in the South. Bells from schools, churches and public buildings were taken and melted down to make cannons. Despite being the king of cotton, there were few textile mills to make bandages, clothing and uniforms. Women took down curtains and scavenged clothing to re-purpose into bandages and clothing. Carpets were made into blankets and mourning dresses would be loaned from house to house among the widows.

The past is prologue in the South's fiscal scenario that we see being repeated these many years later with our own government. The Confederacy needed money to finance its war of secession and printed about 1 billion dollars of unfunded Confederate currency. This devaluation of their currency caused the value of the Confederate dollar to fall to 5 cents by 1864, putting basic necessities and food out of the price range of most southerners. Flour rose to $250 per barrel; corn, $50 a bushel; leather boots, $250 a pair. The anti-Federalists sold its population the British brand free trade and paid a dear price for it.

Southern plantation owners and politicians were not able, or refused to see the effect of increased supply on the price of their cotton. The greatest surprise to planters should have been that it was possible to command the prices it did considering the rapidness of annual increases in production thanks to Eli Whitney's cotton gin. The quantity of cotton produced in 1819 was 88 million pounds; in 1823, 174 million; in 1824, 144 million, and in 1830, nearly 300 million. They failed to grasp that as production of the raw material increased, demand would lower. There were three chief reasons why the consumption of cotton fabrics was greatly increased, and in consequence, the price reduced: 1st, competition; 2nd, the improvement of labor-saving machinery like the cotton gin; and 3rd, the low price of the raw material. The crop of 1819, amounting to 88 million pounds, produced $21 million in revenue; the crop of 1823, amounting to 174 million pounds (almost double that of 1819) produced less money at $20.5 million; and the crop of 1824, amounting to 144 million pounds produced $22.5 million. The State of Georgia was among the few bright spots for manufacturing in the South prior to the breakout of war. The declining cotton prices caused by overproduction fueled investment in manufacturing.

The South's argument that the Morrill Tariff of 1861 was the highest tariff in U.S. history is ironic. The Morrill Tariff was 25.9% in 1863. The Tariff of 1828 that was authored and passed by the Democrats accidentally, because their plan was to put forth a tariff so repugnant, that no one would vote for it, but it passed and their plan backfired and became known as The Tariff of Abominations at 35%. It was not the ushering in of unregulated free trade they had gambled for.

I saw a post that showed a liberal holding up a sign supporting the deportation of Republicans. Could we instead deport the Republican doppelgangers? It's tragic irony how many Americans support societies and internet sites regarding The Federalist Papers. If and when they actually *read* The Federalist Papers, they realize the group they have joined is in direct opposition to the most authoritative exposition on the Constitution ever written.

Whether knowingly or not, many modern self-described conservative Americans support the anti-Federalist agenda. The toothless government experiment has already been played out. It was a spectacular failure. The president of that failed government said that *if* it failed, on its tombstone should be written, "Died of a Theory." That failed government was the Confederacy and the president was Jefferson Davis. He didn't have the power to set aside a day of national prayer without other states refusing to participate and then setting their own separate day of prayer, saying that the president couldn't tell them when to pray. The South had few railroads because of the bickering over right of ways between southern states. They produced little, had limited industry outside of agriculture, and depended heavily on free trade for the finished products they traded raw materials for. While Confederate soldiers were marching shoeless and thread bare, North

Carolina hoarded 92,000 uniforms, saying, they were only for soldiers from their state.

Digging into history—whether it be actual history, or revisionist history, exposes the modern Republican leadership as the old pre-civil war Democrats and modern Democrats as Marxist-Socialists requiring no accountability from government and full accountability and control of the citizenry, while demanding more infrastructure and entitlements in a free trade economy that provides no domestic means of raising the revenue to finance their programs or pay off almost $20,000,000,000,000 in debt. There is no Democrat or Republican Party. There is only the Straw Man Party, or worse, the Free Trade Party and their platform is to race to the bottom to make it cheaper and buy it cheaper from overseas with no respect for quality of work or domestic prosperity.

If we lived by the guidelines of the Federalist Papers, a collection of 85 essays, which Alexander Hamilton was the sole author of 51 and the collaborative author on 20 others, putting his contribution at 71 total, we would still be living in a self-sufficient, sustainable economy with a central government that invested in its infrastructure without the need for income or payroll taxes.

Many Americans held captive by their respective free trade parties would like to bring back the federal government that protected American industry and

American jobs. The first political party that realizes that virtually every working class American will vote for the party that supports domestic industry will win by a landslide—maybe—if they look up from their phones long enough to notice.

It was the opponents of a federal government that brought about the Civil War. The South rightly claims they paid the majority of federal taxes. They paid the most federal taxes through import tariffs because they refused to trade with Northern manufacturers and produced little more than raw materials. They chose rather to fight for free trade with England and Europe and depend on them for manufactured products. Despite the South's refusal to do business with the North, and in the case of South Carolina, even refusing to trade with Kentucky, they paid the most in federal taxes through import tariffs but still made far more profit than their northern manufacturing neighbors due to the competitive advantage that slave labor gave them.

The Northern population in 1860 was approximately 22 million to the South's 9 million—4 million of which were slaves. The conscription act allowed exemptions for men owning over twenty slaves, or permitted the purchase of a substitute, which bred resentment and the feeling among impoverished soldiers that the battle had become "a rich man's war, but a poor man's fight." Many of the Confederate soldiers had no slaves and with no industry in the South for free men, they scratched out their living on family farms. Lack of industry in the south had nothing to do with lack of resources. The South possessed to an extraordinary degree, the most important elements of the manufacturing industry of that time, waterpower and labor. Waterpower alone gave them a distinct advantage over Great Britain; but distrust of slaves and fear that they would sabotage their manufacturing discouraged industries from starting. That was the excuse used for lack of industry in the South. Rather than hire free men, they chose to abstain from manufacturing industries almost altogether because they didn't trust the slaves not to sabotage their factories. Poor free white men of the South had virtually no employment opportunities because of slave labor, yet they *were* the Confederate Army. If Confederate soldiers were not defending slavery, they were most assuredly defending the rights of rich land owning slave owners to continue exploiting slavery at the expense of making poor free white men unemployable.

The makeup of the Union Army included almost every known trade profession from masons, printers, bookbinders, publishers, merchants, politicians, glassblowers, tailors, carpenters, plasterers, iron moulders, puddlers and rollers, blacksmiths, machinists, architects, preachers, doctors, lawyers, teachers, and not least, the agricultural professions.

If sin that is hidden is recognition of guilt; if open slavery is a sin and those that maintain it are criminals; then what is our just reward in this present day where forced labor slavery, seven times greater than that of the 19th century maintains our nation's economic system through free trade?

"The abolitionists would raise the negroes to a social and political equality with the whites. And, that being effected, we would soon see the present condition of the two races reversed. They and their Northern allies would be the masters and we the slaves." — John C. Calhoun

"Those who would deny freedom to others, deserve it not for themselves, and under a just God, cannot long retain it." —Abraham Lincoln

Repeatedly, the argument against the passage of "The Tariff of Abominations" is credited with the smoldering nullification and secession movement, the Tariff of 1828—the tariff that was wholly conceived and established by John C. Calhoun and the South as a means of subterfuge had backfired. The Kentucky Resolutions, written by Thomas Jefferson in the 1790's are often credited and cited as planting the seeds, and used as justification for nullification and secession. The resolution came from Thomas Jefferson's opposition to Alexander Hamilton's American School of economic policies that promoted an industrial nation and protective tariffs, while Jefferson's plan favored an agrarian program and free trade. Thomas Jefferson didn't share Hamilton's vision for the future of U.S. industrial might.

To further bolster the southern argument that the Civil War was about taxation and not slavery, they drew upon the arguments and sympathies of not Americans, but foreign bankers, trading partners, intellectuals and politicians, as if pining for the days of colonialism. Salomon Rothschild of England, wrote at the time, "This state of affairs could have continued ... if the two divisions, South and North, of the Democratic party had not split at the last [1860] electoral convention. Since each of them carried a different candidate, they surrendered power to a third thief, Lincoln, the Republican choice." In another letter, Rothschild wrote, "I'll come back later to the 'slavery' question, which was the first pretext for secession, but which was just a pretext and is now secondary. The true reason which impelled the southern states to secede is the question of tariffs."

Author, Charles Dickens (Yes, that Charles Dickens) of England wrote, "The Northern onslaught upon slavery was no more than a piece of specious humbug designed to conceal its desire for economic control of the southern states." Dickens goes on to say "...Union means so many millions a year lost to the South; secession means the loss of the same millions to the North. The love of money is the root of this as of many other evils... The quarrel between the North and South is, as it stands, solely a fiscal quarrel." Here is a quoted passage from the Northern British Review, Edinburgh, 1862, "...All Northern products are now protected: and the Morrill Tariff is a very masterpiece of folly and injustice. No wonder then that the citizens of the seceding states should feel for half a century they have sacrificed to enhance the powers and profits of the North; and should conclude, after much futile remonstrance, that only in secession could they hope to find redress."

Britain's only motivation for the outcome of the Civil War and siding with the free trade policies of the South, were for its own economic gain and in no way reciprocal toward the South. Britain solely sought advantages to keep the South dependent on Great Britain for their essential supplies. The business model that Britain used in the South was to use its raw materials and in turn sell back clothing and other accommodations, all of which was merchandise manufactured in Great Britain. Their support was nothing more than to maintain the advantages Great Britain had by keeping the South dependent on her for their essential supplies. The southern slave owners had, in effect, made slaves of themselves while simultaneously keeping slaves and impoverishing landless free white men.

I return again to Lord Goderich, addressing another

Member of Parliament:

"It was idle for us to endeavor to persuade other nations to join with us in adopting the principles of what was called 'free trade.' Other nations knew, as well as the noble lord opposite, and those who acted with him, what we meant by 'free trade', was nothing more nor less than, by means of the great advantages we enjoyed, to get a monopoly of all their markets for our manufactures, and to prevent them, one and all, from ever becoming manufacturing nations."

South Carolina lost 15% of its population during the 1820's due to the impoverishment of landless men and runaway slaves. They blamed the Tariff of 1816; they blamed national internal improvements; they blamed competition from cotton producing areas along the Gulf Coast, and they blamed free black sailors from British ships for inciting slave rebellion. They passed the Negro Seamen Act to imprison all free black foreign seamen while their ships were docked in Charleston.

The South's opposition to domestic industry and import tariffs in favor of free trade cannot be divorced from the slavery issue. The myth of free trade and that it promotes the wealth of a nation is a denial of cause and effect. Free trade promotes the wealthy of a nation and not the wealth of a nation. Free trade, slavery and colonialism are inseparable. That evidence is born out to this very day in the impoverishment of the United States, while our shelves are stocked by upwards of 27 million forced labor slaves from Africa, Asia, and elsewhere globally. Just as landless free white men could not compete in wages against slaves and find gainful employment in the pre-Civil War South, Americans today cannot compete with the growing number of foreign low wage labor and forced labor slaves whose products have flooded our nation.

What happened in the South during the 1820's was nothing less than John C. Calhoun and southern slave owners attempting to nullify majority rule. Calhoun didn't want his state to secede, and hoped that nullification would keep South Carolina in the Union while preserving slavery, free trade with Britain, and protection for rich slave owners from unemployable free whites who couldn't compete with slaves. The rich land owners saw themselves as the victims of majority rule and nullification as the means to protect them from Democracy. The Tariff of Abominations had passed and nullification was the next step to protect minority rule in South Carolina. In November, 1832, the South Carolina convention declared the federal tariff laws of 1828 and 1832 null and void in their state. The minority had spoken.

President Jackson secured a Force Bill from Congress and sent troops to reinforce Charleston Harbor in order to maintain majority rule and preserve the union. Much of the derision of Calhoun's plan came from the image he projected of southern land owners as an enslaved minority when they were actually the world's greatest slaveholders with a black to white population ratio of 10 to 1 in portions of the state.

Calhoun, by playing both sides of the issue through the clandestine crafting of the Tariff of 1828 and subsequently labeling it The Tariff of Abominations and calling for nullification, had increased his odds of a favorable outcome. Either nullification would be upheld, granting a victory to the rich minorities, or a compromise would be reached on tariffs. Calhoun succeeded in his bid for a minority win. The majority relented and Congress passed the Compromise Tariff of 1833, partly because most Americans wanted lower tariffs anyway. Calhoun made a speech in 1837 and admitted his part in crafting the Tariff of 1828. The goal was to make tariffs so high that the saboteurs of the bill thought it couldn't possibly pass and would be defeated. In effect, Calhoun had given the minority their victory over the majority, but Congress passed the Force Bill at the behest of President Jackson which compelled South Carolina to comply with federal tariffs under threat of deploying the U.S. Army if they did not comply.

The ethics leading up to the compromise tariff of 1833 were labeled reprehensible, but the well-played victory of South Carolina only emboldened the nullifiers by demonstrating that the North and

Northern anti-nullification Democrats would appease threats and blackmail from the anti-tariff slave owning minority in order to preserve the party and the union. The tactic would be revisited many times within the next thirty years and gave the North time to ponder what might happen to democracy if threats of secession and war were not appeased, and blackmail not paid.

From then until the Civil War, whenever southern extremists sought confrontation, southern moderates would demand concessions from the government, claiming it as patriotic for the preservation of the party and the union. Southern Democrats were far from ignorant of the tool they had fashioned and put it to use against the North, including northern Democrats, turning democracy into a minority rule.

The southern minority demanded a gag rule on all discussion of outlawing slavery in 1835 which resulted in appeasement and The Gag Rule. In 1850, threats arose from the South again, regarding the return of alleged fugitive slaves from the North and promises from extremists to smash the union; a Fugitive Slave Law was passed. In 1854 Southerners demanded repeal of the Missouri Compromise which opened the west to the possibility of enslavement, and they were appeased again.

The War Between the States finally put the majority back in control. From the election of Andrew Jackson until the start of the war, it can't be understated how much power the minority had over the majority. The southern extremists weren't merely a minority. They were a minority of the southern plantation owners, who were a minority of southern Democrats, who were a minority of the Democratic Party. Outrage escalated with each concession made by northern Democrats to the Deep South Democrats, who were the minority of a minority of a minority. The Republican Party grew rapidly in the north due in no small part to the disgust of voters with the Democrats for repeatedly conceding to a sliver of a minority. (1)

The Democratic Party splintered and Abraham Lincoln won the election despite not being on the ballot of ten southern states. By the time Lincoln took the oath of office, five southern states had seceded from the union.

Plantation owners led a pseudo life of aristocracy and *were* the pre-Civil War 1%. Landless and poor free white folks were the 99%. The only life the vast majority would know was a hardscrabble life because there was so little industry in the South and the 99% knew they could never compete with slaves for wages, so why are their descendants so romantic about a confederated nation of states?

Is it because secession romanticists view the old south like many modern day 99 percenters worship present day train wrecks of wealth and fame like the

Kardashians, Real Housewives of Absurdistan and Lifestyles of the Rich. Would their ancestors slap the taste out of their great, great, great grandchildren's mouths if they saw how their offspring live and dared to remember with fondness the life their ancestors endured in competition to slave labor?

I think it's something else. Southerners and those who identify with them emphatically deny the hate message they're labeled with for being proud of their heritage. Their message of "Heritage not hate" falls on deaf ears to opponents who are only too eager to tear down, deface and grind U.S. historical monuments to dust in order to hide history they don't agree with, like ISIS rampaging through the Middle East destroying antiquities. Are Southerners proud because of slavery or in spite of their own hardships endured because of slavery? I think for the 99% the latter might be true.

***

In Defense of The American System

Chapter 6 Common Sense

Before the 2012 presidential election, I wrote a piece about the claims from Mitt Romney that Chrysler was going to start building Jeeps in China. His opponents excoriated him for the claim. He also promised that, if elected, he would label China a currency manipulator on his first day in office. Such a designation is not merely name-calling, but an executive process that could lead to higher tariffs on Chinese goods entering the United States. What did he get for promising to label China a currency manipulator? His own party set out to mob him. (1)

Opponents countered that such tariffs could also trigger a trade war with China. Is there anyone in America who doesn't know that we're already in a trade war with China, and that we're losing, badly? We are perpetually in a trade war with China due to their currency manipulation. Free markets within a protectionist economy encourage consumer buying power through a strong dollar. Free trade with foreign powers, by necessity lowers the value of America's dollar in order to compete with foreign competitors. The primary costs of the falling dollar are higher prices for imported goods and for American tourists traveling abroad. The primary benefit is increased price competitiveness of U.S. products for export. A worthless dollar is great for corporations, especially those who claim to export American goods, but in fact are only packaging and exporting goods they imported from other countries.

There is virtually no import tariff on foreign made automobiles and China is on the verge of selling Chinese vehicles in the U.S., made by factory workers whose total hourly compensation package amounts to $1.88 per hour. Those Chinese vehicles will compete with American automobiles built by Americans whose compensation package averages $35.53 per hour. American made automobiles that are sold in China have tariffs imposed that range from 37 to 42 percent.

President Barack Obama promised to make global warming a top priority in his second term. The most glaring and obvious choice for the greatest impact on the pollution they claim is choking the planet would be to bring industry back to the United States from China, where pollution is so severe that company stock for manufacturers of protective breathing masks has soared because of dirty air that is almost 40 times greater than what the World Health Organization deems a safe limit.

Why do environmentalists not push vigorously for industry to be brought back to the United States where our strict environmental standards would be the greatest weapon against the pollution that is or isn't choking the planet? A factory fire in eastern

China on Monday, January 14, 2012 went unnoticed for three hours because of the thick smog that blanketed the area. After firefighters in Zhejiang province were finally alerted to the blaze, it took ten hours to extinguish the flames.

"Because of the thick fog pervading the air at the time, the initial smoke and flames produced by the fire took almost three hours to be discovered by nearby residents," the Xinhua news agency said.

The dense air pollution across much of China that week reached levels dangerous to human health. At the height of the smog, authorities in the capital said readings for particles small enough to penetrate the lungs, hit 993 micrograms per cubic meter, almost 40 times the World Health Organization's safe limit.

The reduced visibility contributed to a 20-car pileup elsewhere in Zhejiang on Tuesday that left two people dead and eight injured, and forced flights in Beijing to be cancelled according to the Xinhua news agency.

When the eyes of the world were on Beijing for the 2008 Olympics, the Chinese capital implemented strict measures for months beforehand that reduced toxic emissions by 60 per cent. Automobiles could only be used every other day, construction work ceased and factories were shut down. They seeded clouds with dry ice in an attempt to make it rain and clean the air.

Such steps were "extreme resolutions which are not

sustainable", said Professor John Cai, director of the Centre for Healthcare Management and Policy at the China Europe International Business School in Shanghai.

Any doubt that American companies operating in China are there because of the lax environmental standards and slavish wages that the Chinese people work for is nothing short of denial.

The facts minus the spin from the Republicans or Democrats of the reports that Chrysler is planning to make Jeeps in China and may eventually make all products in the Chrysler line over there are 100% factual.

According to Chrysler, they will not close plants in North America. Vehicles sold in the U.S. will still be made in the U.S. Chrysler is however moving to take advantage of the emerging market in China. Chrysler is looking to triple its overseas sales by 2014 to 500,000 units by building Jeeps and possibly the entire Chrysler product line in China for overseas sales based on a Bloomberg report. (2)

How is this a consolation to American automobile workers? Once they were told that Chrysler brand cars that were sold in America would still be made in America, they went back to sleep. They just lost production of 500,000 new American car sales to China and it didn't bother them because they didn't think it affected them. If China can copy and steal our technology, and sell our own products back to us in the form of just about everything we use on a daily basis, why should this give Americans a collective sigh of relief that we are losing the production of U.S. built vehicles sold to China.

Is it inconceivable that Chinese built automobiles with American names that are supposedly being built for Chinese buyers will also make their way into U.S. showrooms? If the profit margin from manufacturing in China and shipping to the United States is high enough, auto manufacturers will absolutely do it.

Jeep sales in China through the month of September, 2012 doubled to 33,463 from what they were for the same period in 2011. The Jeeps currently being sold to China are made in the United States. We will lose all those sales to Chinese production including the possible inclusion of the entire Chrysler product line.

Retaining U.S. plants and domestic sales wasn't a win; it was a huge loss of export sales to China, thanks to their currency manipulation and trade practices. Corporations are what they are and they're going to fall on the side of profit, even if it means exporting their customer's ability to buy their product. The crux is that many, if not the vast majority of corporations don't treat their customers as a renewable resource. A consumer base cannot be maintained if the consumer doesn't have the means to buy your product.

The economics of building a product in the country you're going to be selling it in may make good business sense. We as a nation made no attempt to weight that decision in our favor so that American vehicles sold in China are actually made by Americans. Americans were tainted by politicians and pundits who convinced Americans that they had won and their jobs were safe. Is it unreasonable to demand at the very least, the same protection from our government for our manufacturing jobs as China's industry has for their own?

Our jobs are shipped overseas and we're patronized that those weren't jobs we wanted anyway, because we're just so darn smart. We need to concentrate on tech jobs and let third world countries have those manufacturing jobs that are beneath the pedigree of any self-respecting American, but look where our tech jobs are going, overseas.

The Obama administration claims to have saved GM and the auto industry. They in fact did great harm and at great expense to the American taxpayer. The government did nothing more than take the industry through a managed bankruptcy. A bankruptcy they could have gone through six months sooner and twenty billion dollars cheaper according to many including Mitt Romney.

The government didn't save jobs. It cut jobs, a lot of jobs. I'm not referring to the failed executives of

Detroit or plant workers. The government took the auto industry through bankruptcy and mandated that the companies shut down 2,200 dealerships which put 120,000 people out of work. How many mismanaging corporate executives from the bailed out companies lost their jobs compared to the 2,200 small businesses that employed 120,000 people? Of the 120,000 people that lost their jobs were new car salesmen, used car salesmen, parts counter personnel, lot boys, service managers, service technicians, paint shop employees including painters, body men, collision specialists and parts drivers, finance managers, special finance managers, sales managers, maintenance personnel, secretaries, receptionists, and payroll clerks.

Four out of the top five vehicles purchased through the government's "Cash for Clunkers" program were foreign vehicles, with only Ford, who took no bailout money, breaking the top five. Taxpayers lined the pockets of foreign manufacturers to the tune of three billion dollars whether they took the clunker vouchers or not. "Cash for Clunkers" gave vouchers up to $4500 with the government claiming an average of $4000 over the course of the program. Subtract the number of vehicles that would have been sold anyway during that time period of the 690,000 vehicles sold and you're left with 125,000 credited to "Cash for Clunkers" at a cost of not $4000 per vehicle, but $24,000 per vehicle, of which four out of the top five sellers were foreign vehicles. "Cash for Clunkers" took nearly 680,000 used vehicles off the road, because the government mandated that all used vehicles traded in through the Cash for Clunkers program be destroyed. This significantly drove up used car prices, further gouging taxpayers already paying for vehicles that somebody else is driving. (3) Americans continue to be led like lemmings to foreign auto dealerships believing they are buying quality and that it's ok to buy a foreign car because some of them are assembled in the United States. It may be assembled here but much of the supply chain is not manufactured here. China is criticized for protecting its economy? Should we really criticize China, Germany, etc. for protecting their economy or asking our government why they're not protecting our economy?

I watched automotive reviews about Chinese automobiles and saw how inferior they were to American built cars. No one looking at the inferior build quality of Chinese automobiles should be comforted as if they are not a threat. The competitor clones they built in 2012 that seem inferior are an order of magnitude more advanced than the automobiles they built in 2004. China's auto industry from 2004 produced antique three wheeled meter maid buggies compared to the modern looking vehicles of 2012. They've come that far in eight years.

Where do you think that will put them in another five years? Jeremy Clarkson of BBC's Top Gear put it best when he said, "It seems then, that the term copyright infringement, does not translate terribly well into Mandarin." (4)

Hyundai and Kia are two good examples of imports that went from very poor quality to winning automotive awards in a very short period. If you know someone in the automobile industry from 2004 or so, they can tell you that Hyundai and Kia were terrible cars. The only thing more pathetic than a Hyundai was the look on the owner's face when you told him how much his car was worth at trade in.

There was absolutely nothing original in their design and they were essentially junk. All their designs were based on other vehicles. The Rio was so cheap that if you bought a Kia Sedona, they would give you a Kia Rio for free. I knew the name of very few of them. I called them by the designs they were poorly based on. There was the Hyundai Jaguar, Hyundai Impala, Kia Rav4, etc.

The point is, that was during the mid-2000s'. Now Hyundai has a huge following and I wouldn't be surprised to see them outsell our domestic automobiles or Toyota soon, if they're not already.

The common belief heaved on America is that protectionism is a bad thing, but I would wager that not one person in a hundred could explain why. How can you protect your job if you can't protect your product? Are you going to pay 50% more for an American product when the one next to it from China looks just as good? Some do but many don't, and a glance around the parking lot of any American auto manufacturer's employee parking lot will verify that.

There will be Chinese cars for sale in the United States. I know dealerships that were looking to pick up a line of Chinese built cars as far back as 2006. They're coming and by the time they get here, they'll no longer look like Cushman Trucksters.

It's indisputable that bad things happen in the absence of competition, and that bad thing is called complacency. I listened to some commentators talking about what happened to the American auto industry in the 70s'. One replied that Japan is what happened to the auto industry in the 70s'. I take issue with that. Japan isn't what happened to the auto industry in the 70s'. Detroit is what happened to the auto industry in the 70s'. We built garbage. It wasn't the men and women on the line that built the junk that was sold to us. They built the cars from the designs, and with the materials they were given. It was a corporate decision to build junk. I was a teenager in 1976. Chevrolet made a Bi-Centennial Chevy Vega that had a neat badge with a red, white and blue theme. Since the car was a 76' model, it was no doubt built in 75', meaning, that when I saw it in my high school's auto body shop in the late summer/early fall of 1976, the car couldn't have been more than a year old. It was so eaten out with rust that near basketball size holes were in the quarter panels behind the rear wheels.

The Free Trade policies that have been fought for by Democrat administrations for over 200 years and more recently by both parties with programs like the WTO, GATT, NAFTA, KORUS, and soon, the Trans Pacific Partnership which are all endorsed by Republicans, have killed countless manufacturing jobs in this country and in return our government patronizes us with mind persuasion, "These aren't the jobs you're looking for."

Our founding fathers believed in protecting our economy. Alexander Hamilton was the father of the "American School" of economics which advocated protectionism. The three main articles of which were;

1. Support industry by advocating protectionism and opposing free trade through protection from foreign competition in the form of tariffs.

2. Create infrastructure to support commerce and industry with roads and railroads.

3. Create financial infrastructure with a National Bank promoting the growth of productive enterprises rather than speculation.

The U.S. economy grew to be the largest in the world with Americans having the highest standard of living while using the American system. Democrats repeatedly tried to repeal it until the system was essentially gone by the 1970's. Woodrow Wilson, a Democrat, did as much as any president to disassemble the American system by removing tariffs and replacing the National Bank with the Federal Reserve. It was speculation by the Federal Reserve System and not the Smoot-Hawley Tariff Act that eventually led to the stock market crash of 1929 and the Great Depression. Federal Reserve chairman, Ben Bernanke, finally admitted in 2012, that the Federal Reserve caused the Great Depression, but he said they were sorry and that it wouldn't happen again.

President George H. W. Bush pushed for and signed the North American Free Trade Agreement on December 17, 1992 along with Mexican President Carlos Salinas and Canadian Prime Minister Brian Mulroney. It was a top priority for President Bill Clinton and signed into law on December 8, 1993. President Ronald Reagan as far back as 1984 campaigned for a North American common market.

Since America was born, the Democrat Party which evolved from anti-Federalist factions that opposed Alexander Hamilton's fiscal policies of protectionism have tried to open our borders to free trade. The anti-Federalist factions evolved into the Democratic-Republican Party that eventually became the Democrat Party. The Democrat Party opposed a national bank and wealthy moneyed interest. They supported free trade with other countries and were pro-slavery.

The Republican Party was formed from the Whig Party and from anti-slavery Democrats. They supported a national bank and protection of domestic industry and jobs from foreign competition, until they eventually joined forces with the Democrats in 1913.

Today no one is protecting domestic industry but the deception played on the American people by Democrats and Republicans alike is insulting while they give pandering accolades about American productivity knowing fully how much of our current productivity comes from foreign made goods that are shipped back to the United States before they are sold domestically or overseas and counted as overall productivity.

The insult is made worse by politicians and pundits who blame unemployment on American productivity and those over-productive workers that are stifling job growth. There's nothing coincidental about corporate profits rising to record highs at the same time there was a 100% increase in unemployment.

My niece sent me information about a group of conservatives, the Wilberforce Agenda. It's a group of conservatives who focus on issues like human trafficking, including forced prostitution and forced labor slavery. The purpose is to form a strategic agenda aimed at conservatives who are turned off by the unfavorable image portrayed of them in areas such as caring for the unborn, with no regard for children after they're born. They have a brilliant agenda, but there are potentially two major hurdles in their agenda that oligarchs will oppose vigorously. Eliminating human trafficking and promoting internet freedom in countries with tight controls over what information is available to their citizens is a tough sale to multi-national corporations that are puppeteers for many of our politicians. The elimination of human trafficking would throw a wrench into the free trade slavery dictum of comparative advantage and/or absolute advantage. Internet freedom for people living in countries without it would threaten corporate plantation overseers with uprisings from their forced labor slaves, but—no matter, because the Wilberforce Agenda was short-lived and their website no longer exists.

Alexander Hamilton was murdered by an anti-federalist, confederate—and traitor, but the American School of economics lived on. He is still feared by free traders over 200 years after his death. The same factions that shame liberal extremists for wanton destruction of Confederate history are removing defenders of the American System from our national landscape. Alexander Hamilton is being replaced on the ten dollar bill and President McKinley's namesake

Mount McKinley has been renamed Denali.

"If the people were not tainted with the spirit of their State representatives, they, as the natural guardians of the Constitution, would throw their weight into the national scale and give it a decided preponderancy in the contest." — Alexander Hamilton

The number of Americans on food stamps has skyrocketed from 13 million in June, 2008 to over 46 million people in June, 2012 for an increase of over 350%. Our population is 313,232,044 by July, 2012 estimates. A staggering 21% of Americans qualify for legal aid and government assistance. That means 46 million people on food stamps must be supported by 128 million working Americans. For every 11 Americans still employed, the task falls on them to support 4 Americans on food stamps, plus take care of their own family needs.

The government has made great strides against population growth and immigration. Five million jobs were created since January, 2009 for a net loss of four million with population growth and assuming 2011-2012 figures will be the same as they were the two previous years. Population growth is down nearly a half million for the two year period of 2009-2011. Population growth from July, 2010 to July, 2011 dropped 200,000 compared to two years before. Immigration was down 150,000 for the same period because job opportunities are not here. This is the flattest growth since "The Great Depression".

***

In Defense of The American System

Chapter 7 The Way We Were

I've heard it said, that the last time you could buy a gallon of gasoline for a quarter was in the 1950's, but I remember buying gasoline for a quarter in the 1960's. The average price for a gallon of regular unleaded gasoline in America is $3.66 in 2013, but the average price in 2003 was $1.56. For 52 years, the price of gasoline from 1919 to 1971 averaged around $0.25 per gallon. The last year that quarters were made of 90% silver was 1964; meaning, that if we were still under the gold standard, you could buy regular unleaded gasoline in 2013 for $0.16 per gallon instead of $3.66. That's the reality of abandoning the gold standard and the rampant devaluation of America's money supply by the Federal Reserve.

Gold and silver is money; Federal Reserve paper is not money; its currency. The exorbitant price of gold and silver today is not an indicator of the precious metal's worth, but a standard by which the worthlessness of Federal Reserve paper can be measured.

In 2013, Ben Bernanke backed away from claims that the Federal Reserve was going to start shrinking the balance sheet by selling Treasury Bonds. The Fed's refusal to quit printing money, while continuing to paper over the economy only further indicates their commitment to the myth of free trade and the skydiving game of chicken between the U.S. dollar and foreign currencies, with the Fed determined to open our chute last in order to have the most worthless currency. The Federal Reserve has no exit strategy for a self-sustaining U.S. economy, but to the contrary, has created an economy that is dependent on government stimulus to bloat the money supply and debt in order to compete in the race to the bottom of the global free trade currency war.

There's an old analogy that tries to explain why people accept bad policy with little or no protest. The boiling frog anecdote describes a frog slowly being boiled alive. The premise is that if a frog is placed in hot water, it will jump out, but if it's placed in cold water that is slowly heated, it won't perceive the danger and will be cooked to death. Reality appears to contradict the anecdote, as it relates to modern Americans. The forefathers of our nation had less tolerance for political and economic shenanigans from Great Britain; else there may not have been a revolution. The length of time allowed to pass before colonists revolted against perceived danger, would appear to be confined to a timeframe of immediately, or sooner, compared to what Americans in modern society are willing to bear.

Britain might still retain rights to America, had it given representation to the colonies, but as history accurately attests, though the colonies were of great significance to Britain for its resources, they were necessary only for the transfer of America's wealth to Britain. There was no representation for the American colonies in British government. After the French and Indian War, Britain needed revenue to pay for the Seven Years' War, as it was named. The Stamp Act was passed by British Parliament on March 22, 1765 with an effective date of November 1, 1765. The purpose of the tax was partly to help pay for troops stationed in North America after the British won the Seven Years' War. The British government claimed that the colonies were the primary beneficiaries of a military presence and should pay a portion of the expense. The Stamp Act of 1765 required that many printed materials in the colonies be on stamped paper that was only produced in London, carrying an embossed revenue stamp. The printed materials that were required to carry the stamp weren't isolated to legal documents, but also to newspapers, magazines and other types of paper. The paper had to be paid for in British currency, and not in colonial paper currency.

Though Britain did want the colonists to pay for the forces stationed in the colonies, the tax served a more diabolical purpose, as a fee charged to inmates to pay for the maintenance of the prison guards watching over them. In an attempt to keep the colonies subservient and unlearned, the highest taxes were levied against lawyers and college students to limit the growth of a professional class in the colonies. To protest, the colonies made a voluntary agreement to not import anything from England until the Stamp Act was repealed. It was repealed almost a year to the day after it was made effective, on March 18, 1766.

Opposition to the Tea Act of 1773 was more immediate and one of the last nails in the coffin of British rule in America. Rebellion against the Tea Act wasn't about high taxes, because in fact, it made legally imported tea from the East India Company cheaper than smuggled Dutch tea. The British Constitution made it illegal to tax citizens without the permission of its representatives, but the colonists had no representatives in British Parliament. The argument of the protesters was that there could be no taxation without representation. The purpose of the Tea Act was to give a government created monopoly to the East India Company, and it was feared the government may give future monopolies for other products. The colonists learned the details of the Tea Act while seven ships were in route for America with East India Tea. Four of the ships were in route to Boston and one each to New York, Philadelphia and Charleston. Protesters in every colony but Massachusetts were able to prevent the ships from unloading and forced the tea to be returned to England. Loyalist Massachusetts Governor Tom

Hutchison was determined to stand his ground, and would not let the ships leave. On the evening of December 16, 1773, a group of men dressed in Mohawk warrior disguises, boarded the three docked ships and dumped hundreds of chests of tea into the water. The fourth ship that was to arrive in Boston encountered a storm on the way and was lost at sea.

In modern America, we not only tolerate taxation without representation, we give it our sanction. While Republicans and Democrats play the politics of misdirection with their willing media accomplices, Americans focus on everything they're told to concentrate on except the problem, jobs. Multinational corporate lobbyists write legislation for trade agreements that invade our domestic policy and create new corporate power that is passed by our elected officials.

Both parties are complicit in the deception when the Right claims that job creators are being punished, while the Left claims that everything can be fixed by making the rich pay their fair share. Neither party will address the issue of actual job creation because their agenda of free trade has no mechanism for creating meaningful employment opportunity within the United States.

Republicans are the self-proclaimed champions and defenders of the job creators that Democrats call the evil 1%. Do these job creators actually create jobs in

America? If so, then by all means quit taxing them altogether. Let's not make them the 1%; make them the 0.01%. Under the American System, job creators were paid bounties.

Only 3 to 10 percent of the nation's money supply is in physical currency, which is backed by nothing, so where is the other 90%? How much is made out of electronic material consisting of ones and zeros on a computer screen and backed by a material less tangible than air, faith?

Is there any benefit to be had by pointing out the obvious, that jobs are shipped overseas, our currency is devalued, and no conspiracy is needed to cover it up because Americans don't care? Attempts are made on our First Amendment rights under the Constitution by both parties as they invent wedge issues with limited but increasing success. There is no truly effective wedge to divide the American people in order to take their attention away from the theft of our sovereignty until the Second Amendment is threatened. While some remain fixated on fabricated wedge issues of amendments to the Bill of Rights, the overriding principle of the Constitution is ignored, specifically, our responsibility to establish Justice, insure domestic tranquility, provide for the common defence, promote the general welfare, and secure the blessings of liberty to ourselves and our posterity. Arguments are abundant over interpretation of the

Constitution, but free trade runs counter to it in such an overwhelming manner, that blinders cannot hide it. Democrats think the problem can be solved by taxing the rich and giving other people's money away to the poor—after a small finder's fee of course. Washington taxes and regulates businesses into oblivion, and then calls them unpatriotic for not putting up with it and leaving.

Rick Santorum wants to keep the Export/Import Bank. The Congressional Budget Office says the bank is a loser. That means that we're making other nations rich to the tune of $500 billion dollars annually, and on top of that, we're paying other countries to buy our stuff. So, we forfeit a half trillion dollars to other nations for being the biggest loser in the free trade game. And, since we feel so bad for losing, we forfeit another 200 million dollars annually through the Export/Import Bank—because we're good losers and nobody likes a sore loser.

I do love the Bush family, and I know beyond doubt that they love this country. I get weepy every time I watch George H. W. Bush get pulled out of that raft and up onto the rescue sub after he was shot down in WWII. But, when Jeb says that his plan will raise the revenue the government needs to make things better—I cry for another reason.

We the People of the United States, in Order to form a more perfect Union, establish Justice, insure domestic

Tranquility, provide for the common defence, promote the general Welfare, and secure the Blessings of Liberty to ourselves and our Posterity, do ordain and establish this Constitution for the United States of America. (1)

The British free trade system does not fulfill one premise of our guarantees under the Constitution. The American System was and can be again, the vehicle by which we can fulfill our guarantees in the Constitution, to ourselves and our posterity.

***

In Defense of The American System

Chapter 8 A Rising Tide Raises All Ships

A favorite quote from free trade advocates is, "A rising tide raises all ships." Conveniently left out of this analogy is that when the tide is high in parts of the world that have taken our manufacturing, it beaches us here.

If the American System had been defeated before the emancipation of slaves, humans would likely as not still be property in America. Does that sound extreme? Since free trade didn't defeat the American System until years after the emancipation proclamation, we now keep our current 27 million forced labor slaves hidden overseas.

The American System would virtually banish slave made goods sold to America. It's already illegal to import goods to our country that are slave made and yet forced labor slavery continues to grow. People in third world countries that actually collect a paycheck subsist on dirt wage compensation.

Because of the lop-sided free trade model we are forced to live and compete under now, (which for the sake of this argument is the textile and clothing industry) it costs $13.22 to produce a denim shirt in America yet the same shirt can be produced in Bangladesh for $3.72 according to a CNN report from May, 2013. (1)

Under our current free trade model, there is virtually

no room left for the Bangladeshi manufacturer to lower his costs because his labor cost for producing this shirt is $0.22 leaving very little room for wage cuts, unless of course he switches to slave labor which would raise the number of forced labor slaves in the world above the already astronomical number of 27 million. Americans would still not have jobs in this sector because we can't compete on wages with slave labor, much less paid labor at $0.22 per hour. The last time I checked, the Bangladeshi minimum wage was actually $0.18 per hour.

The Bangladeshi manufacturer can't cut corners in his factory because it's already crumbling and outfitted with antiquated equipment.

Bear with me while I go into my pipedream and eliminate slavery worldwide and offer a system that will raise all ships. Under an economic model similar to the American System or a tariff based system, or if you please, a fair trade system, American jobs would be protected from competing with slave made goods. If it cost $13.22 to make a shirt in America and Bangladeshis can make the same shirt for $3.72, there would be a $9.50 tax at the border which would go into our government's coffers.

The American System could end slave made goods feeding our global supply chain just as it did in the South over 150 years ago. Consider the Bangladeshi manufacturer as if he were competing under an economic model similar to the American System. He would profit nothing by undercutting American manufacturers through the exploitation of his employees. No matter how cheaply he produces his goods, he must pay a tax for the difference in price of his cheaply made denim shirt compared to the American made denim shirt. Why would he pay the US government $9.50 to sell a shirt that only cost him $3.72 to make? He would be more competitive if he gave that money to his employees and invested in state of the art factory equipment instead of barring the doors and locking his employees inside death factories that have claimed hundreds of lives in numerous factory fires in Bangladesh, including 500 deaths from one factory fire alone in 2013.

If the Bangladeshi manufacturer's cost rises $9.00 higher than his current rate, he now has modern equipment and a paid labor force working for a livable wage. His tax at the US border drops from $9.50 to merely $0.50 and best of all for America, U.S. workers are competing on a level playing field with their foreign competition instead of losing jobs to dirt wage or worse, human slaves working under horrid conditions. Thank you for your patience. That concludes my pipedream.

The Obama administration intends to fight ISIS with a jobs program for terrorists. It was thought to be a gaffe when State Department spokeswoman Marie

Harf said that jobs would make Islamic militants turn away from terrorism. When ISIS beheaded 21 Egyptian Christians she said, "We cannot win this war by killing them, we cannot kill our way out of this war. We need to go after the root causes that lead people to join these groups, whether it's lack of opportunity or jobs."

There is however a glimmer of truth. The world is not withholding economic opportunity from Muslims who live under the thumb of Islamic terrorists. It's the terrorists who withhold opportunity from their own people. Neutralize the terrorists and the economy of these regions will right itself. When Arabs under a terrorist regime begin to exhibit economic independence through free markets, terrorists will thwart it.

Gaza is an excellent example. No jobs program will ever fix Gaza until the terrorists are removed. Israel unilaterally withdrew from Gaza in 2005. Gaza's geographical location is excellent for economic growth and stability. Gaza is situated on the Mediterranean Sea and close to the Suez Canal. Within a year Hamas took over the government in Gaza. The Hamas rise to power led to security restrictions placed on the borders by Israel. Gaza relies heavily on exports for its economy but the private sector has almost collapsed since Hamas took over the government. There are high rates of poverty and unemployment. Gaza by 2012 should have been a thriving economic territory but after Hamas took power in 2006 they announced they would refuse to honor past agreements between the Palestinian government and Israel.

In 2010 Israel eased it closure policy on Gaza borders which resulted in an economic upturn. This led to wide scale economic development including industry and the building of malls, hotels and an increase in the import of cars. The increase was so dramatic that there was a shortage of construction workers which resulted in Gaza sending young people to Turkey to learn trades.

Citizens with jobs, self-respect, money, cars, homes and financial security might be less likely to enlist as screaming jihadists with bombs strapped to their chest running for the Israeli border to massacre the infidels. Hamas felt they needed to start another war before the citizens of Gaza got too comfortable. A Muslim with nothing to live for and no prospects for improvement is probably easier to manipulate than a Muslim who can securely provide for their family and their welfare.

Hamas holds the citizens and economy of the Gaza Strip hostage and blames Israel for its plight while the population has to rely on outside assistance from the UN and other humanitarian agencies.

Democrats and Republicans alike talk about the

economic opportunities that have opened up in Cuba. It's important to understand what this could mean for manufacturers currently operating from thousands of miles away. President Obama just pulled off something that the current generation of Republicans have only dreamt about, but Republicans are way out of their league. Democrats have been opening up corridors to slave and dirt wage human resources long before Republicans were even called Republicans. Cuba is an eleven million strong population of domesticated, clever, supremely resourceful, (thanks to their abject poverty) and ready to go workforce that can bring overseas manufacturing back from Asia's forced labor slaves and dirt wage laborers and plant it 90 miles off our shore. The Cuban people are a great people with brilliant problem solving skills and ingenuity that is long lost by many Americans—not because Americans can't learn these skills, but because they're not taught. The reason being; the jobs that teach these skills aren't available. Americans don't want to develop ingenuity and problem solving skills the same way the Cubans did—the same way our depression era parents and grandparents did.

The rationale behind normalizing relations with Cuba is presented as, "if we don't do it the Russians will." That reasoning carries as much logic as the reluctant looter's quandary, that if he doesn't take the television, someone else will.

When Marco Rubio seemed to stand alone against the normalization of relations with Cuba, my heart skipped. Could he be the first president since Warren G. Harding to attempt a return to the American System? He had to know how attractive the opportunity was to American corporations with factories overseas. The logistics involved in getting product from the design table to market is complicated by thousands of miles between the factory and the consumer, the shipping costs, the language barrier, and the turnaround time for design changes or defects just to name a few of the problems. My hopes were dashed once I learned of his support for the Trans Pacific Partnership, which includes re-training for American workers that will lose their jobs.

Segments of the Tea Party were aware and warning of the potential dangers of the Trans Pacific Partnership as far back as 2012. This is the same treaty that Boehner and Obama wanted to "Fast Track". Fast Track is not just a term; fast tracking means that congress agrees to give up its authority under the Constitution to study and debate the trade deal. Fast Track means a simple up or down vote without study or debate of the free trade agreement. Politicians influenced by corporate lobbyists are the ones that pushed for Fast Track status. They include the same politicians that rightly condemned Nancy Pelosi for telling America they would have to pass the Affordable Care Act before they would tell us what was in it. They're two sides of the same bad penny.

Obama stated four times in the 2015 State of the Union address that "Globalization" had devastated American manufacturing and then followed it by saying that he wanted to "Fast Track" new Asia-Pacific partnerships to cure the problem, specifically meaning the Trans Pacific Partnership or TPP. I couldn't believe my ears. I immediately had an image of TPP architects sitting together watching the State of the Union address. Their breath catches as they hear the same words I hear; applause erupts from the Democrats and Republicans in the House of Representatives where the address is held. After they picked their dropped jaws from the floor, the knee slapping and guffawing among the friends of TPP must have been riotous.

They listened to the president lay out the damage wrought by free trade not once, but four times, followed by promising more of the same while the congress cheered. The exhilaration must have been like a near death experience for those who desperately want more free trade deals for America.

"Did you hear that?"

"I—I did. I did hear him say that—didn't I?"

"Holy Moses, he just told them four times that

globalization had destroyed American manufacturing and then told them that he was going to give them more globalization, and they cheered; they cheered."

"Wow, he's good... uh... phuh... umm... I can't make words."

"No one will stop us now."

It remains to be seen if the TPP will right America's listing ship. Unfounded fear over another free trade deal after a long string of disappointments would be a very welcome change.

If the idea of slavery being the most important link in our global supply chain doesn't stir your righteous indignation, I get it, you're probably normal. Because really, judging by the popularity of Walmart and its kind, who cares? But even the simplest life form possesses a sense of self-preservation. Why does our sense of self-preservation not extend to our ability to make a living? Oh, you're a school teacher and the government signs your paycheck, so lost manufacturing jobs don't really affect you, right? Lost tax revenue from coal mines has resulted in the closure of many schools. In Boone County, WV, 2698 coal miners have lost their jobs over a three year period. Factor in the indirect employment multiplier that adds 1.4 jobs per every manufacturing job according to the Bureau of Labor Statistics and that number jumps from 2698 lost coal mining jobs to 6475 total jobs lost. The additional 3777 indirect job losses related to the industry can and does devastate whole communities. Three schools in Boone County are on a closure list as of October, 2015. You may say that coal died from government regulation and not as a result of free trade, and you would be right—and wrong. Many of these displaced coal miners migrated into the oil and gas mining industry as demand for natural gas increased due to coal fired power plants converting from coal to natural gas. They lost their jobs again when we allowed our nation to be flooded with oil and gas from the Middle East.

Let's tax the businesses that sent all our jobs overseas as punishment for their greed—that's what a good socialist would do, right? Wrong; a business isn't going to pay a punitive tax bill; the president of the company isn't going to pay a punitive tax bill; the shareholders of the company aren't going to pay a punitive tax bill. You and I will pay that bill because the cost will be passed on to us. If your Uncle Rasputin falls in a grocery store and sues; the store doesn't pay for that; the customers do. Tax a business and you tax the working class.

The definition of provincialism is narrowness of mind, ignorance, or the like, considered as resulting from lack of exposure to cultural or intellectual activity. "I can't believe Nixon won. I don't know anyone who voted for him." This quote is attributed to New Yorker film critic Pauline Kael, and seems a fair analysis of the media's lack of understanding regarding the motivation behind the support of disgruntled Americans for Donald Trump. On some level, any of the media's rationale regarding Trump support will be true. Some will support him because they agree with everything he says or hang on every word. Some will support Trump because of his immigration policy, celebrity status, bombast, etc.

Is the news media so provincial; so far removed from the plight of blue collar Americans that they can report with a straight face that Donald Trump's popularity is due to his celebrity, or any of the other wild claims of his appeal instead of the real reason? Donald Trump is not popular with Americans because of his bombast and political incorrectness. He's popular in spite of it, specifically because of his stance on America's lop-sided trade deals. The media credits virtually everything but his stance on our trade deals for Donald Trump's popularity. Blue collar Americans have suffered the simultaneous pandering and condescension of politicians for decades regarding manufacturing losses. People have always known politicians are liars of varying degrees, but the well of trust has been bailed dry.

Print news media vs online news sources is an example of competition and innovation. Brick and mortar stores vs online retailers is an example of competition and innovation. American workers in safe factories making a living wage vs Bangladeshis in crumbling death traps making $0.18 an hour is neither about competition nor innovation. The American System is the system; and the tide that can truly raise all ships.

***

In Defense of The American System

Chapter 9 Versus

There are a few ways to sell a product; tell the truth and let the product stand on its own record and merit—and another way. Here is the British System free trade sales pitch, from typical claims by senior economic policy analysts followed by a rebuttal in defense of the American System.

New technologies bring about change, as the history of the U.S. economy shows, benefits society as a whole. It's normal for some economic sectors to suffer while adapting to the new changes before the benefit shows. The Americans that are suffering in certain economic sectors such as manufacturing is really the result of new technologies challenging the old methods of production.

For the sake of debate, give legitimacy to the claim that Americans in the manufacturing sector are suffering because new technologies are challenging the old methods of production. What possible adaptation to the new changes must take place in order for the benefit to show? Adaptation to automation, resulting in increased efficiency, quality, productivity and ease of interchangeability of parts for the purpose of repair and replacement have been taking place in America since Eli Whitney invented the assembly line in 1797. The "division of labor" is not the conception of Adam Smith. The Venetian Arsenal in Venice Italy used this practice in the 16th century to build galley ships at a rate of one ship per day. The Chinese demonstrated the division of labor with the production of 8000 terracotta figures we know as the Terracotta Army buried with the first emperor of China in 210 B.C. The adaptation that has yet to take place for suffering Americans in the manufacturing sector, is to the exportation of the U.S. manufacturing base to third world countries.

NAFTA was signed into law in 1993 and went into effect on January 1, 1994. Foreign goods and services as a percentage of U.S. GDP in 1993 was 11%. The United States has since advanced every free trade agreement possible while foreign goods and services as a percentage of U.S. GDP rose to 18% in 2011. The average unemployment rate for 1994 was 6% vs. an average of 9.6% for 2011. The U.S. lost more than 56,000 factories from 2001 to 2010. If economic statistics are correct, approximately 1 million jobs are displaced for every 80 billion dollars in trade deficit. Our trade deficit was $324 billion in 2013, amounting to a displacement of more than 4.1 million U.S. jobs.

The most compelling reason to support free trade is that society as a whole benefits from it. Free trade increases the standard of living of people because it allows them to buy quality goods at lower prices.

Since free trade was wholly embraced in the 1990's, Henry Clay's prediction of poverty limiting our consumption to bare subsistence is coming true before our eyes. To paraphrase President William McKinley, it's claimed that free trade makes things cheaper. Whether an item is cheap or expensive depends on what we can earn by our labor. Free trade cheapens a product by cheapening the worker that makes the product. Protectionism cheapens the product by elevating the worker that makes the product. Free trade advocates say, buy where you can buy the cheapest. Protectionists say, buy where you can pay the easiest. (1)

The establishment of domestic manufacturers creates jobs and excites the creation of wealth, and this gives new powers of consumption, which are gratified by the purchase of foreign objects. A poor nation can never be a great consuming nation. Its poverty will limit its consumption to bare subsistence.

New technologies and innovation are born when competition from the challenge of others who produce similar products and services motivates companies to find new technologies and better ways to provide what they produce.

Wealth created by protectionism drove technology and competition in the United States for scores of years. The recent unfettered reign of free trade has driven Americans back to agrarianism as farm prices soar. Many Americans under financial pressure are also learning to grow their own food. Seed and plant sales from 2008 to 2009 went up 30%, as well as canning supplies and sewing products as more people are learning how to sew, while being labeled, "economic survivalists", as if their poverty were a political statement of anarchism.

Increased productivity from free trade competition fosters economic growth by lowering production costs and raising the standard of living of ordinary Americans.

Competition within the borders of a protectionist nation with a free market the size of America saw continuous lowering of production costs as each generation was predictably able to raise their standard of living higher than that of their parents. Purchasing power for 90% of income earners has not increased for 20 years. Inflation from 1990 to 2010 was 51.8%. Median household income fell $5000 from 2008 to 2012 while inflation rose 6.5% for the same period. According to the Bureau of Labor Statistics, the labor force participation rate is lower in 2015 than any time since the 1970s'.

Subsidies and special protections benefit small economic interests or sectors at the expense of millions of consumers and producers. They translate into higher prices, the impact of which is felt primarily by poor Americans.

This is a red herring, because bad protectionist policy is as catastrophic as free trade. The easiest example is U.S. sugar protection. Candy makers in America, by law must use domestic sugar, but Mexico's sugar is half the price. The result is that candy makers have moved their factories to Mexico en masse. Global free trade and bad protectionist policies cannot be mixed. Free markets within protectionist borders have consistently lowered the price of goods and services in the United States.

When facing competition from Chinese manufacturing, U.S. manufacturers have two options: either adopt new technologies to cut costs and become more competitive or shift the focus of their operations to different areas in which they can be more competitive. Neither of these two options harms consumers, since they will continue to have access to the least expensive, best-quality products.

The new technologies under the guise of free trade have been adopted, and they're being used in China and anywhere there is a ready supply of low wage labor and forced labor slaves. Corporations have indeed shifted the focus of their operation to different areas—geographically shifting their operations to third world countries. Manufacturing is responsible for 80% of the goods traded in America. Exactly what knowledge based industry are these tens of millions of manufacturing laborers going to migrate to for the paychecks to buy these less expensive, best-quality products? Domestic companies can create empires by selling a can of beer for $0.50, but shoe manufacturers using low wage or forced labor slaves charge $135.00 for a pair of dress shoes, claiming they cannot make a profit making shoes domestically.

Most workers benefit as well. For some people, free trade requires change, but they also now have opportunities to use their skills in more efficient, advantageous, and productive ways that are created by the innovation and prosperity that competition promotes.

Innovation and competition are not the singular domain of third world countries with a forced labor slave workforce. America's free market within our economically protected borders made us without peer the most efficient, productive, innovative, competitive, and prosperous nation on earth. America was the first nation to have a broad working middle class—America invented the working middle class, as opposed to the European middle class that was comprised of a small sliver of intellectuals and professionals.

Free trade fosters an enormous chain of economic activity, the benefits of which culminate in a social desire to be at peace with neighboring and even faraway nations with which trade is conducted or might be conducted in the future. The areas of the Middle East in which civil wars and terrorist havens abound are both economically repressed and mostly unfree.

What is the net benefit for America, from the free trade missionary crusade of freedom? Americans have willingly, almost eagerly surrendered personal freedoms in the name of security. Representatives have been derelict in discussing the constitutionality of infringing liberties as each new security measure is taken in stride while simultaneously apologizing for the terrorists. There is a hint of truth however. America sits at peace with many countries while turning a blind eye to the nations who use any number of the 27 million human trafficked laborers that feed our global supply chain, keep our store shelves stocked, and our labor force unemployed.

In the 1980s, personal computers were very expensive, few people owned them, and those they did own handled only word texts and a few calculations. Due to increased competition, by 2002, 65.9 percent of people living in the United States owned a personal computer that handled text, calculations, graphics, media, internet access, and many other functions.

Personal computers were expensive because they were a *new* technology, just as every new technological achievement is expensive. Printers that print 3D objects are currently prohibitively expensive, but as the technology advances, the price will continue to fall, as it already is falling, until they're affordable enough to be in every home that has a computer and laser jet printer. They'll no doubt eventually be bundled with PC's like conventional printers are often done now. Competition with forced labor slaves in Malaysian computer factories isn't responsible for the technological achievements of today's computers; Americans are.

The benefits of the lower value of the dollar will be felt predominantly in the manufacturing sector, as it accounts for more than 80% of traded goods in the United States. This means that the positive effects of the falling dollar are concentrated in the sector that has suffered most in the recent recession.

The most prized possession of free trade advocates is a worthless dollar. Before the Federal Reserve and its speculative practices replaced the National Bank in 1913, a dollar had the buying power of $1.75. Multiply that times the current domestic manufacturing compensation package of $35.53 and compensation for American manufacturing would be worth $62.17 an hour. Unfortunately, the dollar's value has dropped from $1.75 to $0.05 or less since the Federal Reserve took over our money supply in 1913. A compensation package of $35.53 per hour is comparable to $1.77 since the Fed took over. The dollar is nearly worthless now and America lost manufacturers at a rate of over 15 per day from 2001 to 2010.

The Administration should lower the tax and regulatory burden on U.S. companies so that they can be more competitive. Moving toward greater, not less, economic freedom benefits all Americans.

When America protected our borders economically before the Federal Reserve, and free trade rose from the ashen hole it was cast into with the defeat of the

Confederacy, there was no income or payroll tax. Up to 95 percent of our government's budget was covered by protective trade tariffs from our beginning when America was dependent on many imports, all the way past the point we overtook Great Britain in the industrial revolution and Americans had a higher standard of living than any nation on earth, but I don't think that's the tax break free trade advocates are asking for.

For over a century, free trade has been one of the most important determinants of America's wealth and strength.

Which century is that? Does that century include the future? The future normally wouldn't count as credit for this claim unless your company's name is Enron. The foundation for free trade was laid in 1913 with the enactment of income and payroll taxes, and the Federal Reserve, but the backwardness of competition and the decimation caused by two world wars kept many import manufacturers away from our shores until the mid to late 1950's when the first European and Asian import automobiles started showing up in dealerships.

The United States is losing ground on economic freedom because other countries are freeing their markets at a faster pace than the U.S.

Which countries have the most economic freedom due to the blistering pace of freeing their markets compared to America? Japan's trade barriers allowed

1 Chevrolet for every 400 Toyotas imported into the United States in 2008. American automakers have no plants in Japan. Ford sold 2,500 vehicles to Korea compared to 330,000 imported to the U.S. from Hyundai and Kia. This doesn't include foreign auto factories in America, which are primarily plants that assemble the parts manufactured in their respective foreign countries.

U.S. manufacturers think it is unfair that labor in China is cheaper than labor in the United States, and therefore ask for tariffs against Chinese products. But those tariffs would, in reality, be unfair to millions of U.S. consumers and producers who would be forced to pay higher prices for locally manufactured goods.

I and a lot of Americans don't think it's a stretch to claim that—our free trade agreements have saved us so much money, we're broke.

***

In Defense of The American System

Chapter 10 Henry Clay

Henry Clay's 1832 speech is the inspiration for this book. He gave his emotional and effective three day speech on the floor of the Senate titled, "In Defense of the American System", on the days of February 2, 3, and 6, 1832. The "American System" that Mr. Clay defended, evolved from Alexander Hamilton's "American School". Although Henry Clay's oratory style was different than many of his counterparts, he was without peer in speech delivery. I don't think it's bold to say that one can almost hear his words as they're read.

One of Henry Clay's fiercest opponents during his career was the famous senator from South Carolina, John C. Calhoun, who once said, "I don't like Clay... I wouldn't speak to him, but, by God! I love him."

If any man ever had the background and motivation to lend his support to our modern slave driven economic supply chain, it would have been the famous senator from West Virginia, Robert C. Byrd.

Senator, Robert C. Byrd, from my State of West Virginia, was known as the "Soul of the Senate", a statesman, a defender of the Constitution, respected historian, and—it must be admitted, a former member of the Ku Klux Klan in the 1940's. He held more leadership posts than any other senator, cast more votes than any other senator, and served longer than any other senator. Senator Byrd explained in his last autobiography that he was a member of the KKK because he "was sorely afflicted with tunnel vision—a jejune and immature outlook—seeing only what I wanted to see because I thought the Klan could provide an outlet for my talents and ambitions." He also said, in 2005, "I know now I was wrong. Intolerance had no place in America. I apologized a thousand times... and I don't mind apologizing over and over again. I can't erase what happened." He had this to say about Senator Henry Clay of Kentucky:

From the nation's earliest days, Congress has struggled with the fundamental issue of the national government's proper role in fostering economic development. Henry Clay's "American System", devised in the burst of nationalism that followed the War of 1812, remains one of the most historically significant examples of a government-sponsored program to harmonize and balance the nation's agriculture, commerce, and industry. This "System" consisted of three mutually reinforcing parts: a tariff to protect and promote American industry; a national bank to foster commerce; and federal subsidies for roads, canals, and other "internal improvements" to develop profitable markets for agriculture. Funds for these subsidies would be obtained from tariffs and sales of public lands. Clay argued that a vigorously maintained system of sectional economic interdependence would eliminate the chance of renewed subservience to the free-trade, laissez-faire "British System." In the years from 1816 to 1828, Congress enacted programs supporting each of the American System's major elements. After the 1829 inauguration of President Andrew Jackson's administration, with its emphasis on a limited role for the federal government and sectional autonomy, the American System became the focus of anti-Jackson opposition that coalesced into the new Whig party under the leadership of Henry Clay.

Henry Clay has been aptly labeled "the most influential member" of the Senate during its golden age of the 1830's and 1840's. His personal Magnetism—his passionate, charming, and ingratiating manner, made Clay one of America's best-loved politicians; but his consuming ambition for the presidency led him to compromise his principles in a series of major blunders that frustrated those public figures and private citizens who sought his forceful leadership. One biographer concluded that "there was a serious statesman in him along with the gamester-politician; behind his never-ending series of plausible expedients there was a consistency of purpose. Clay has been overrated as a politician and underrated as a statesman."

The Kentuckian took his first Senate oath of office in 1806 at age twenty-nine, despite being three months under the constitutionally required age for membership. Filling out an unexpired term, he served less than three months, and in January 1810 he returned for another brief period. Moving to the House of Representatives in 1811, Clay was chosen Speaker on his first day in that body, a post he held intermittently for a decade. He served as Secretary of State in John Quincy Adams' administration, and following Andrew Jackson's 1828 defeat of Adams, Clay returned to the Senate in November 1831. Within months, the National Republican party nominated Clay to oppose Jackson in the 1832 election.

Clay's move to the Senate in 1831 symbolized the increasing prestige of the upper chamber, which was rapidly becoming the principal theater for the nation's intensifying legislative battles.

Early in 1832, as the Jackson administration moved closer to paying off its national debt, Clay recommended abolishing tariffs on foreign goods that did not compete with American products. This would have obvious political appeal to the purchasers of those goods and would reduce the flow of revenue into the treasury, preventing Jackson from extinguishing the debt in time to take credit for it in the 1832 election campaign. Southerners who hated protective tariffs argued that Clay's reductions were inadequate.

By 1831, the Kentucky senator enjoyed a national reputation as an outstanding orator. A book entitled *The Speeches of Henry Clay* had appeared four years earlier, the first such volume to be published in the United States and [an indication of] the importance parliamentary eloquence had attained in the nation's life. Clay's oratorical power, unlike that of Webster, lay not in his choice of words or extent of his knowledge, but in his style of delivery. Raised in a western tradition that valued oratory for its entertainment rather than educational value, Clay tailored his remarks for a wide audience, filling them with popular allusions while omitting the learned quotations that other classical orators favored. Unlike Calhoun, who delivered scholarly addresses with a maximum of speed and a minimum of ornamentation, Clay adopted a deliberative style that made effective use of calculated pauses, well-timed body gestures, and simple direct arguments. Carl Schurz, who served in the Senate in the 1870's with those who had known Clay, believed the Kentuckian possessed "the true oratorical temperament, that force of nervous exaltation that makes the orator feel himself, and appear to others, a superior being, and almost irresistibly transfuses his thoughts, his passions, and his will into the mind and heart of the listener."

On February 2, 1832, Clay used the first speech of his

Senate career to launch a major attack on the Jackson administration. This three-day speech, entitled "In Defense of the American System", focused principally on the importance of maintaining protective tariffs, despite complaints of such southern spokesmen as Senator Robert Y. Hayne of South Carolina and Vice President John C. Calhoun that they would ruin the region's economy.

Historian Merrill Peterson reconstructed the image Clay conveyed to his audience during delivery of this address. "The chamber was packed to hear the man whose powers of persuasion—now charming, now badgering; now beseeching, now deprecating; now subdued, now vehement—were legendary, and who, if he did not command assent by the strength of his views, won it with his captivating manner and seductive voice." Friends and foes alike admired the sound of Clay's voice. Another scholar concludes, "His voice was a magnificent instrument to express his emotions and ideas, remarkable clear, at times soft as a lute and other times full as a trumpet, beautifully modulated." (1)

The last chapter of this book contains Henry Clay's three-day speech in February, 1832, in its entirety, "In Defense of the American System." Henry Clay's speech is to the American System what The Federalist Papers are to the Constitution.

In Defense of The American System

***

In Defense of The American System

Chapter 11 Henry Clay's Speech

Henry Clay

In Defense of the American System

February 2, 3, and 6, 1832

(In the Senate)

In one sentiment, Mr. President, expressed by the honorable gentleman from South Carolina (1), though, perhaps not in the sense intended by him, I entirely concur. I agree with him that the decision on the system of policy embraced in this debate involves the future destiny of this growing country. One way, I verily believe, it would lead to deep and general distress, general bankruptcy, and national ruin, without benefit to any part of the Union. The other, the existing prosperity will be preserved and augmented, and the nation will continue rapidly to advance in wealth, power, and greatness, without prejudice to any section of the confederacy
Thus viewing the question, I stand here as the humble but zealous advocate, not of the interests of one state, or seven states only, but of the whole Union. And never before have I felt more intensely the overpowering weight of that share of responsibility

which belongs to me in these deliberations. Never before have I had more occasion than I now have, to lament my want of those intellectual powers, the possession of which might enable me to unfold to this Senate, and to illustrate to this people, great welfare of my country. I should, indeed, sink, overwhelmed and subdued, beneath the appalling magnitude of the task which lies before me, if I did not feel myself sustained and fortified by a thorough consciousness of the justness of the case which I have espoused, and by a persuasion, I hope not presumptuous, that it has the approbation of that Providence who has so often smiled upon these United States.

Eight years ago, it was my painful duty to present to the other house of Congress an un-exaggerated picture of the general distress pervading the whole land. We must all yet remember some of its frightful features. We all know that the people were then oppressed and borne down by an enormous load of debt; that the value of property was at the lowest point of depression; that ruinous sales and sacrifices were everywhere made of real estate; that stop laws and relief laws and paper money were adopted to save the people from impending destruction; that a deficit in the public revenue existed, which compelled government to seize upon, and divert from its legitimate object, the appropriation to the sinking fund, to redeem the national debt; and that our commerce and navigation were threatened with a complete paralysis. In short, sir, if I were to select any term of seven years since the adoption of the present Constitution, which exhibited a scene of the most widespread dismay and desolation, it would be exactly that term of seven years which immediately preceded the establishment of the tariff of 1824.

***

Existing State of Unparalleled Prosperity

I have now to perform the more pleasing task of exhibiting an imperfect sketch of the existing state of the unparalleled prosperity of the country. On a general survey, we behold cultivation extended, the arts flourishing, the face of the country improved, our people fully and profitably employed, and the public countenance exhibiting tranquility, contentment, and happiness. And if we descend into particulars, we have the agreeable contemplation of a people out of debt; land rising slowly in value, but in a secure and salutary degree; a ready, though not extravagant market for all the surplus productions of our industry; innumerable flocks and herds browsing and gamboling on ten thousand hills and plains, covered with rich and verdant grasses; our cities expanded, and whole villages springing up, as it were, by enchantment; our exports and imports increased and increasing; our tonnage, foreign and coastwise, swelling and fully occupied; the rivers of our interior animated by the perpetual thunder and lightning of countless steamboats; the currency sound and abundant; the public debt of two wars nearly redeemed; and, to crown all, the public treasury overflowing, embarrassing Congress, not to find subjects of taxation, but to select the objects which shall be liberated from the impost. If the term of seven years were to be selected of the greatest prosperity which this people have enjoyed since the establishment of their present Constitution, it would be exactly that period of seven years which immediately followed the passage of the tariff of 1824. This transformation of the condition of the country from gloom and distress to brightness and prosperity, has been mainly the work of American legislation, fostering American industry, instead of allowing it to be controlled by foreign legislation, cherishing foreign industry. The foes of the American System, in 1824, with great boldness and confidence, predicted, 1st. The ruin of the public revenue, and the creation of a necessity to resort to direct taxation. The gentleman from South Carolina, (2) I believe, thought that the tariff of 1824 would operate a reduction of revenue to the large amount of eight millions of dollars. 2nd. The destruction of our navigation. 3rd. The desolation of commercial cities. And 4th. The augmentation of the price of objects of consumption, and further decline in that of the articles of our exports. Every prediction which they made has failed—utterly failed. Instead of the ruin of the public revenue, with which they then sought to deter us from the adoption of the American System, we are now threatened with its subversion, by the vast amount of the public revenue produced by that system. Every branch of our navigation has increased. As to the desolation of our cities, let us take, as an example, the condition of the largest and most commercial of all of them, the great northern capital. I have in my hands the assessed value of real estate in the city of New York, from 1817 to 1831. This value is canvassed, contested, scrutinized, and adjudged, by the proper sworn authorities. It is therefore, entitled to full credence. During the first term, commencing with 1817, and ending in the year of the passage of the tariff of 1824, the amount of the value of real estate was, the first year, $57,799,435, and after various fluctuations in the intermediate period, it settled down at $52,019,730, exhibiting a decrease, in seven years of $5,779,705. During the first year of 1825, after the passage of the tariff, it rose, and, gradually ascending throughout the whole of the latter period of seven years, it finally, in 1831, reached the astonishing height of $95,716,485! Now, if it be said that this rapid growth of the city of New York was the effect of *foreign commerce*, then it was not correctly predicted, in 1824, that the tariff would destroy foreign commerce, and desolate our commercial cities. If, on the contrary, it be the effect of internal trade, then internal trade cannot be justly chargeable with the evil consequences imputed to it. The truth is, it is the joint effect of both principles, the domestic industry nourishing the foreign trade, and the foreign commerce, in turn, nourishing the domestic industry. Nowhere, more than in New York, is the combination of both principles so completely developed. In the progress of my argument I will consider the effect upon the price of commodities, produced by the American System, and show that the very reverse of the prediction of its foes, in 1824, has actually happened.

Whilst we thus behold the entire failure of all that was foretold against the system, it is a subject of just felicitation to its friends, that all their anticipations of its benefits have been fulfilled, or are in progress of fulfillment. The honorable gentleman from South Carolina has made an allusion to a speech made by me, in 1824, in the other house, in support of the tariff, and to which, otherwise, I should not have particularly referred. But I would ask anyone, who could now command the courage to peruse that long production, what principle there laid down is not true? What prediction then made has been falsified by practical experience?

It is now proposed to abolish the system to which we owe so much of the public prosperity, and it is urged that the arrival of the period of the redemption of the public debt has been confidently looked to as presenting a suitable occasion to rid the country of the evils with which the system is alleged to be fraught. Not an inattentive observer of passing events, I have been aware that, among those who were most eagerly pressing the payment of the public debt, and, upon

that ground, were opposing appropriation to other great interests, there were some who cared less about the debt than the accomplishment of other objects. But the people of the United States have not coupled the payment of *their* public debt with the destruction of the protection of *their* industry, against foreign laws and foreign industry. They have been accustomed to regard the extinction of the public debt as relief from burden, and not as the infliction of a curse. If it is to be attended or followed by the subversion of the American System, and an exposure of our establishments and our productions to the unguarded consequences of the selfish policy of foreign powers, the payment of the public debt will be the bitterest of curses. Its fruit will be like the fruit
Of that forbidden tree, whose mortal taste
Brought death into the world, and all our wo,
With loss of Eden.
If the system of protection be founded on principles erroneous in theory, pernicious in practice—above all, if it be unconstitutional, as is alleged, it ought to be forthwith abolished, and not a vestige of it suffered to remain. But, before we sanction this sweeping denunciation, let us look a little at this system, its magnitude, its ramifications, its duration, and the high authorities which have sustained it. We shall see that its foes will have accomplished comparatively nothing, after having achieved their present aim of

breaking down our iron foundries, our woollen, cotton, and hemp manufacturings, and our sugar plantations. The destruction of these would undoubtedly lead to the sacrifice of immense capital, the ruin of many thousands of our fellow citizens, and incalculable loss to the whole community. But their prostration would not disfigure, nor produce greater effect upon the *whole* system of protection, in all its branches, than the destruction of the beautiful domes upon the Capitol would occasion to the magnificent edifice, which they surmount. Why, sir, there is scarcely an interest, scarcely a vocation in society, which is not embraced by the beneficence of this system.

It comprehends our coasting tonnage and trade, from which all foreign tonnage is absolutely excluded.

It includes all our foreign tonnage, with the inconsiderable exception made by treaties of reciprocity with a few foreign powers.

It embraces our fisheries, and all our hardy and enterprising fishermen.

It extends to almost every mechanic art: to tanners, cordwainers, tailors, cabinetmakers, hatters, tinners, brass-workers, clock-makers, coach-makers, tallow-chandlers, trace-makers, rope-makers, cork-cutters, tobacconists, whip-makers, paper-makers, umbrella-makers, glass-blowers, stocking-weavers, button-makers, saddle and harness-makers, cutlers, brushmakers, bookbinders, dairymen, milk-farmers, blacksmiths, type-founders, musical instrument-makers, basket-makers, milliners, potters, chocolate-makers, floor-cloth makers, bonnet-makers, hair-cloth makers, copper-smiths, pencil-makers, bellows-makers, pocket book-makers, card-makers, glue-makers, mustard-makers, lumber-sawyers, saw-makers, scale-beam-makers, scythe-makers, wood-saw-makers, and many others. The mechanics enumerated enjoy a measure of protection adapted to their several conditions, varying from 20 to 50 percent. The extent and importance of some of these artisans may be estimated by a few particulars. The tanners, curriers, boot and shoe-makers, and other workers in hides, skins, and leather, produce an ultimate value per annum of $40 millions; the manufacturers of hats and caps produce an annual value of $15 millions; the cabinetmakers, $12 millions; the manufacturers of bonnets and hats for the female sex, artificial flowers, combs, etc., $7 millions; and the manufacturers of glass $5 millions.

It extends to all lower Louisiana, the delta of which might as well be submerged again in the Gulf of Mexico, from which it has been a gradual conquest, as now to be deprived of the protecting duty upon its great staple. It affects the cotton planter (3) himself, and the tobacco planter, both of whom enjoy protection.

The total amount of the capital vested in sheep, the land to sustain them, wool, woollen manufactures, and woollen fabrics, and the subsistence of the various persons directly or indirectly employed in the growth and manufacture of the article of wool, is estimated at $167 million, and the number of persons at 150,000.

The value of iron, considered as a raw material, and of its manufactures, is estimated at $26 million per annum. Cotton goods, exclusive of the capital vested in the manufacture, and of the cost of the raw material, are believed to amount, annually, to about $20 million.

These estimates have been carefully made by practical men, of undoubted character, who have brought together and embodied their information. Anxious to avoid the charge of exaggeration, they have sometimes placed their estimates below what was believed to be the actual amount of these interests. With regard to the quantity of bar and other iron annually produced, it is derived from the known works themselves; and I know some in western states which they have omitted in their calculations.

Tariff History

Such are some of the items of this vast system of protection, which it is now proposed to abandon. We might well pause and contemplate, if human imagination could conceive the extent of mischief and ruin from its total overthrow, before we proceed to the work of destruction. Its duration is worthy, also, of serious consideration. Not to go behind the Constitution, its date is coeval with that instrument. It began on the ever memorable 4th day of July—the 4th day of July, 1789. The second act which stands recorded in the statute book, bearing the illustrious signature of George Washington, laid the cornerstone of the whole system. That there might be no mistake about the matter, it was then solemnly proclaimed to the American people and to the world, that it was *necessary for* "the encouragement and *protection of* manufactures," that duties should be laid. It is in vain to urge the small amount of the measure of protection then extended. The great principle was then established by the fathers of the Constitution, with the Father of his Country at their head. And it cannot now be questioned, that, if the government had not then been new and the subject untried, a greater measure of protection would have been applied, if it had been supposed necessary. Shortly after, the master minds of Jefferson and Hamilton were brought to act on this interesting subject. Taking views of it appertaining to the departments of foreign affairs and of the treasury, which they respectively filled, they presented, severally, reports which yet remain monuments of their profound wisdom, and came to the same conclusion of protection to American industry. Mr. Jefferson argued that foreign restrictions, foreign prohibitions, and foreign high duties, ought to be met, at home, by American restrictions, American prohibitions, and American high duties. Mr. Hamilton, surveying the entire ground, and looking at the inherent nature of the subject, treated it with an ability which, if ever equalled, has not been surpassed, and earnestly recommended protection.

The wars of the French revolution commenced about this period, and streams of gold poured into the United States through a thousand channels, opened or enlarged by the successful commerce which our neutrality enabled us to prosecute. We forgot, or overlooked, in the general prosperity, the necessity of encouraging our domestic manufactures. Then came the edicts of Napoleon, and the British orders in council; and our embargo, nonintercourse, nonimportation, and war, followed in rapid succession. These national measures, amounting to a total suspension for the period of their duration, of our foreign commerce, afforded the most efficacious encouragement to American manufactures; and, accordingly, they everywhere sprung up. Whilst these measures of restriction and this state of war continued, the manufacturers were stimulated in their enterprises by every assurance of support, by public sentiment, and by legislative resolves. It was about that period (1808) that South Carolina bore her high testimony to the wisdom of the policy, in an act of her legislature, the preamble of which, now before me reads: "Whereas the establishment and *encouragement of* domestic manufactures is conducive to the interest of a State, by adding new *incentives to industry*, and as being the means of disposing, to advantage, the surplus productions of the *agriculturist*; And whereas, in the present unexampled state of the world, their establishment in our country is not only *expedient*, but politic, in rendering us *independent of* foreign nations." The legislature, not being competent to afford the most efficacious aid, by imposing duties on foreign rival articles, proceeded to incorporate a company.

Peace, under the treaty of Ghent, returned in 1815, but there did not return with it the golden days which preceded the edicts levelled at our commerce by Great Britain and France. It found all Europe tranquilly resuming the arts and the business of civil life. It found Europe no longer the consumer of our surplus, and the employer of our navigation, but excluding, or heavily burdening, almost all the productions of our agriculture; and our rivals in manufactures, in navigation, and in commerce. It found our country, in short, in a situation totally different from all the past—new and untried. It became necessary to adapt our laws, and especially our laws of impost, to the new circumstances in which we found ourselves. Accordingly, that eminent and lamented citizen, then at the head of the treasury, (Mr. Dallas) (4) was required, by a resolution of the House of Representatives, under date the 23rd day of February, 1815, to prepare and report to the succeeding session of Congress a system of revenue conformable with the actual condition of the country. He had the circle of a whole year to perform the work, consulted merchants, manufacturers, and other practical men, and opened an extensive correspondence. The report which he made at the session of 1816, was the result of his inquiries and reflections, and embodies the principles which he thought applicable to the subject. It has been said that the tariff of 1816 was a measure of mere revenue; and that it only reduced the war duties to a peace standard. It is true that the question then was, how much and in what way, should the double duties of the war be reduced? Now, also the question is, on what articles shall the duties be reduced so as to subject the amount of the future revenue to the wants of the government? Then it was deemed an inquiry of the first importance, as it should be now, how the reduction should be made, so as to secure proper encouragement to our domestic industry. That this was a leading object in the arrangement of the tariff of 1816, I well remember, and it is demonstrated by the language of Mr. Dallas. He says, in his report,

There are few, if any Governments, which do not regard the establishment of domestic manufactures as a chief object of public policy. The United States have always so regarded it... The demands of the country, while the acquisition of supplies from foreign nations was either prohibited or impracticable, may have afforded a sufficient inducement for this investment of capital, and this application of labor; but the inducement, in its necessary extent, must fail, when the day of competition returns. Upon that change in the condition of the country, the preservation of the manufacturers, which private citizens, under favorable auspices, have constituted the property of the nation, becomes a consideration of general policy, to be resolved by a recollection of past embarrassments; by the certainty of an increased difficulty of reinstating upon any emergency, the manufactures which shall be allowed to perish and pass away, etc.

The measure of protection which he proposed was not adopted, in regard to some leading articles, and there was great difficulty in ascertaining what it ought to have been. But the *principle* was then distinctly asserted, and fully sanctioned.

The subject of the American System was again brought up in 1820, by the bill reported by the chairman of the Committee on Manufactures, now a member of the bench of the Supreme Court of the United States, (5) and the principle was successfully maintained by the representatives of the people; but the bill which they passed was defeated in the Senate. It was revived in 1824, the whole ground carefully and deliberately explored, and the bill then introduced, receiving all the sanctions of the Constitution, became the law of the land. An amendment of the system was proposed in 1828, to the history of which I refer with no agreeable recollections. The bill of that year, in some of its provisions, was framed on principles directly adverse to the declared wishes of the friends of the policy of protection. I have heard (without vouching for the fact) that it was so framed, upon the advice of a prominent citizen, now abroad, with the view of ultimately defeating the bill, and with assurances that, being altogether unacceptable to the friends of the American System, the bill would be lost. Be that as it may, the most exceptionable features of the bill were stamped upon it, against the earnest remonstrances of the friends of the system, by the votes of southern members, upon a principle, I think, as unsound in legislation as it is reprehensible in ethics. The bill was passed, notwithstanding, it having been deemed better to take the bad along with the good which it contained, than reject it altogether. Subsequent legislation has corrected very much the error then perpetrated, but still that measure is vehemently denounced by gentlemen who contributed to make it what is was.

Thus, sir, has this great system of protection been gradually built, stone upon stone, and step by step, from the 4th of July, 1789, down to the present period. In every stage of its progress it has received the deliberate sanction of Congress. A vast majority of the people of the United States has approved, and continues to approve it. Every chief magistrate of the United States, from Washington to the present, in some form or other, has given to it the authority of his name; and, however the opinions of the existing president are interpreted south of Mason and Dixon's line, on the north they are, at least, understood to favor the establishment of a *judicious tariff*.

The question, therefore, which we are now called upon to determine, is not whether we shall establish a new and doubtful system of policy, just proposed, and for the first time presented to our consideration; but whether we shall break down and destroy a long established system, patiently and carefully built up, and sanctioned, during a series of years, again and again, by the nation and its highest and most revered authorities. And are we not bound deliberately to consider whether we can proceed to this work of destruction without a violation of the public faith? The people of the United States have justly supposed that the policy of protecting *their* industry, against *foreign* legislation and *foreign* industry, was fully settled, not by a single act, but by repeated and deliberate acts of government, performed at distant and frequent intervals. In full confidence that the policy was firmly and unchangeably fixed, thousands upon thousands have invested their capital, purchased a vast amount of real and other estate, made permanent establishments, and accommodated their industry. Can we expose to utter and irretrievable ruin this countless multitude, without justly incurring the reproach of violating the national faith?

I shall not discuss the constitutional question. Without meaning any disrespect to those who raise it, if it be debatable, it has been sufficiently debated. The gentleman from South Carolina suffered it to fall unnoticed from his budget; and it was not until after he had closed his speech and resumed his seat, that it occurred to him that he had forgotten it, when he again addressed the Senate, and, by a sort of protestation against any conclusions from his silence, put forward the objection. The recent free trade convention at Philadelphia, it is well known were divided on the question; and although the topic is noticed in their address to the public, they do not *avow* *t*heir own *belief th*at the American System is unconstitutional, but *represent th*at *such is* the opinion of respectable portions of the American people. Another address to the people of the United States, from a high source, during the past year, treating this subject, does not *assert th*e opinion of the distinguished author, but *states th*at of others to be that it is unconstitutional. From which I infer that he did not, himself, believe it unconstitutional.

[Here the Vice President (6) interposed, and remarked that if the Senator from Kentucky alluded to him, he must say that his opinion was, that the measure was unconstitutional.]

When, sir, [said Mr. CLAY] I contended with you, side by side, and with perhaps less zeal than you exhibited, in 1816, I did not understand you then to consider the policy forbidden by the Constitution.

[The Vice President again interposed, and said that the constitutional question was not debated at that time, and that he had never expressed an opinion contrary to that now intimated.]

I give way with pleasure, [said Mr. CLAY] to these explanations, which I hope will always be made when I say anything bearing on the individual opinions of the chair. I know the delicacy of the position, and sympathize with the incumbent, whoever he may be.

It is true, the question was not debated in 1816; and why not? Because it was not debatable; it was then believed not fairly to arise. It never has been made, as a distinct, substantial, and leading point of objection. It never was made until the discussion of the tariff of 1824 (7) when it was rather hinted at, as against the *spirit of* the Constitution, than formally announced, as being contrary to the provisions of that instrument. What was not dreamt of before, or in, 1816, and scarcely thought of in 1824, is now made by excited imaginations, to assume the imposing form of a serious constitutional barrier.

Benefits to all Sections

Such are the origin, duration, extent, and sanctions of the policy which we are now called upon to subvert. Its beneficial effects, although they may vary in degree, have been felt in all parts of the Union. To none, I verily believe, has it been prejudicial. To the North, everywhere testimonies are borne to the high prosperity which it has diffused. There, all branches of industry are animated and flourishing. Commerce, foreign and domestic, active; cities and towns springing up, enlarging and beautifying; navigation fully and profitably employed, and the whole face of the country smiling with improvement, cheerfulness, and abundance. The gentleman from South Carolina has supposed that we, in the West, derive no advantages from this system. He is mistaken. Let him visit us, and he will find, from the head of La Belle Riviere, at Pittsburgh, to America, at its mouth the most rapid and gratifying advances. He will behold Pittsburgh itself, Wheeling, Portsmouth, Maysville, Cincinnati, Louisville, and numerous other towns, lining and ornamenting the banks of that noble river, daily extending their limits, and prosecuting, with the greatest spirit and profit, numerous branches of the manufacturing and mechanic arts. If he will go into the interior, in the state of Ohio, he will there perceive the most astonishing progress in agriculture, in the useful arts, and in all the improvements to which they both directly conduce. Then let him cross over into my own, my favorite state, and contemplate the spectacle which is there exhibited. He will perceive numerous villages, not large, but neat, thriving, and some of them highly ornamented; many manufactories of hemp, cotton, wool, and other articles. In various parts of the country, and especially in the Elkhorn region, and endless succession of natural parks; the forests thinned; fallen trees and undergrowth cleared away; large herds and flocks feeding on luxuriant grasses; and interspersed with comfortable, sometimes elegant mansions, surrounded by extensive lawns. The honorable gentleman from South Carolina says that a profitable trade was carried on from the West, through the Saluda gap, in mules, horses, and other livestock, which has been checked by the operation of the tariff. It is true that such a trade was carried on between Kentucky and South Carolina, mutually beneficial to both parties; but, several years ago, resolutions, at popular meetings, in Carolina, were adopted, not to purchase the produce of Kentucky, by way of punishment for her attachment to the tariff. They must have supposed us as stupid as the sires of one of the descriptions of the stock of which that trade consisted, if they imagined that their resolutions would affect our principles. Our drovers cracked their whips, blew their horns, and passed the Saluda gap, to other markets, where better humors existed, and equal or greater profits were made. I have heard of your successor in the House of Representatives, (8) Mr. President, this anecdote; That he joined in the adoption of those resolutions, but when, about Christmas, he applied to one of his South Carolina neighbors to purchase the regular supply of pork for the ensuing year, he found that he had to give two prices for it; and he declared if *that* *were* the patriotism on which the resolutions were based, he would not conform to them, and, in point of fact, laid in his annual stock of pork by purchase from the first passing Kentucky drover. That trade, now partially resumed, was maintained by the sale of the western productions on the one side, and Carolina money on the other. From that condition of it, the gentleman from South Carolina might have drawn this conclusion, that an advantageous trade may exist, although one of the parties it pays in specie for the productions which he purchases from the other; and, consequently, that it does now follow, if we did not purchase British fabrics, that it might not be the interest of England to purchase our raw material of cotton. The Kentucky drover received the South Carolina specie, or, taking bills, or evidences of deposit in the banks, carried these home, and disposing of them to the merchant, he brought out goods, of foreign or domestic manufacture, in return. Such is the circuitous nature of trade and remittance, which no nation understands better than Great Britain.

Nor has the system, which has been the parent source of so much benefit to other parts of the Union, proved injurious to the cotton growing country. I cannot speak of South Carolina itself, where I have never been, with so much certainty; but of other portions of the Union in which cotton is grown, especially those bordering on the Mississippi, I can confidently speak. If cotton planting is less profitable than it was, that is the result of increased production; but I believe it to be still the most profitable investment of capital of any branch of business in the United States. And if a committee were raised, with power to send for persons and papers, I take upon myself to say that such would be the result of the inquiry. In Kentucky, I know many individuals who have their cotton plantations below, and retain their residence in that state, where they remain during the sickly season; and they are all, I believe, without exception, doing well. Others, tempted by their success, are constantly engaging in the business, whilst scarcely any comes from the cotton region to engage in western agriculture. A friend, now in my eye, a member of this body, upon a capital of less than seventy thousand dollars, invested in a plantation and slaves, made, the year before last, sixteen thousand dollars. A member of the other house, I understand, who, without removing himself, sent some of his slaves to Mississippi, made last year, about 20 percent. Two friends of mine in the latter state, whose annual income is from thirty to sixty thousand dollars, being desirous to curtail their business, have offered estates for sale, which they are willing to show, by regular vouchers of receipt and disbursement, yield 18 percent per annum. One of my most opulent acquaintances, in a country adjoining to that in which I reside, having married in Georgia, has derived a large portion of his wealth from a cotton estate there situated.

The loss of the tonnage of Charleston, which has been dwelt on, does not proceed from the tariff; it never had a very large amount, and it has not been able to retain what it had, in consequence of the operation of the principle of free trade on its navigation. Its tonnage has to the more enterprising and adventurous tars of the northern states, with whom those of the city of Charleston could not maintain a successful competition in the freedom of the coasting trade existing between the different parts of the Union. That this must be the true cause, is demonstrated by the fact, that, however it may be with the port of Charleston, our coasting tonnage, generally, is constantly increasing. As to the foreign tonnage, about one-half of that which is engaged in the direct trade between Charleston and Great Britain is English; proving that the tonnage of South Carolina cannot maintain itself in a competition under the free and equal navigation secured by our treaty with that power.

Free Trade

When gentlemen have succeeded in their deign of an immediate or gradual destruction of the American System, what is their substitute? Free trade! Free trade! The call for free trade, is as unavailing as the cry of a spoiled child, in its nurse's arms, for the moon or the stars that glitter in the firmament of heaven. It never has existed; it never will exist. Trade implies at least two parties. To be free, it should be fair, equal, and reciprocal. But if we throw our ports wide open to the admission of foreign productions, free of all duty, what ports, of any other foreign nation, shall we find open to the free admission of our surplus produce? We may break down all barriers to free trade on our part, but the work will not be complete until foreign powers shall have removed theirs. There would be freedom on one side, and restrictions, prohibitions, and exclusions, on the other. The bolts, and the bars, and the chains, of all other nations will remain undisturbed. It is, indeed possible that our industry and commerce would accommodate themselves to this unequal and unjust state of things: for such is the flexibility of our nature, that it bends itself to all circumstances. The wretched prisoner, incarcerated in a jail, after a long time, becomes reconciled to his solitude, and regularly notches down the passing days of his confinement.

Gentlemen deceive themselves. It is not free trade that they are recommending to our acceptance. It is, in effect, the British colonial system that we are invited to adopt; and, if their policy prevail, it will lead substantially to the re-colonization of these states, under the commercial dominion of Great Britain. And whom do we find some of the principal supporters, out of Congress, of this foreign system? Mr. President, there are some foreigners who always remain exotics, and never become naturalized in our country: whilst, happily, there are many others who readily attach themselves to our principles and our institutions. The honest, patient, and industrious German readily unites with our people, establishes himself upon some of our fat land, fills his capacious barn, and enjoys, in tranquility, the abundant fruits which his diligence gathers around him, always ready to fly to the standard of his adopted country, or of its laws, when called by the duties of patriotism. The gay, the versatile, the philosophic Frenchman, accommodating himself cheerfully to all the vicissitudes of life, incorporates himself, without difficulty, in our society. But, of all foreigners, none amalgamate themselves so quickly with our people as the natives of the Emerald Isle. In some of the visions which have passed through my imagination, I have supposed that Ireland was, originally, part and parcel of this continent, and that, by some extraordinary convulsion of nature, it was torn from America, and drifting across the ocean, was placed in the unfortunate vicinity of Great Britain. The same openheartedness; the same generous hospitality; the same careless and uncalculating indifference about human life, characterize the inhabitants of both countries. Kentucky has been sometimes called the Ireland of America. And I have no doubt that, if the current of emigration were reversed, and set from America upon the shores of Europe, instead of bearing from Europe to America, every American emigrant to Ireland would there find, as every Irish emigrant here finds, a hearty welcome and a happy home!

But sir, the gentleman to whom I am about to allude, (9) although long a resident of this country, has no feelings, no attachments, no sympathies, no principles, in common with our people. Near fifty years ago, Pennsylvania took him to her bosom, and warmed, and cherished, and honored him; and how does he manifest his gratitude? By aiming a vital blow at a system endeared to her by a thorough conviction that it is indispensable to her prosperity. He has filled, at home and abroad, some of the highest offices under this government, during thirty years, and he is still at heart an alien. The authority of his name has been invoked, and the labors of his pen, in the form of a memorial to Congress, have been engaged, to overthrow the American System, and to substitute the foreign. Go home to your native Europe, and there inculcate upon her sovereigns your Utopian doctrines of free trade, and when you have prevailed upon them to unseal their ports, and freely admit the produce of Pennsylvania, and other states, come back, and we shall be prepared to become converts, and to adopt your faith.

A Mr. Sarchet also makes no inconsiderable figure in the common attack upon our system. I do not know the man, but I understand he is an unnaturalized emigrant from the island of Guernsey, situated in the channel which divides France and England. The principle business of the inhabitants is that of driving a contraband trade with the opposite shores, and Mr. Sarchet, educated in that school, is, I have been told, chiefly engaged in employing his wits to elude the operation of our revenue laws, by introducing articles at less rates of duty than they are justly chargeable with, which he effects by varying their denominations, or slightly changing their forms. This man, at a former session of the Senate, caused to be presented a memorial signed by some 150 pretended workers in iron. Of these, a gentleman made a careful inquiry and examination, and he ascertained that there were only about 10 of the denomination represented; the rest were tavern keepers, porters, merchants' clerks, hackney coachmen, etc. I have the most respectable authority, in black and white, for this statement.

[Here Mr. HAYNE asked, who? and was he a

manufacturer? Mr. CLAY replied, Colonel Murray, of New York, a gentleman of the highest standing for honor, probity, and veracity; that he did not know whether he was a manufacturer or not, but the gentleman might take him as one. (10)]

Whether Mr. Sarchet got up the late petition presented to the Senate from the journeymen tailors of Philadelphia, or not, I do not know. But I should not be surprised if it were a movement of his, and if we should find that he has *cabbaged from* other classes of society to swell out the number of signatures.

To the facts manufactured by Mr. Sarchet, and the theories by Mr. Gallatin, there was yet wanting one circumstance to recommend them to favorable consideration, and that was the authority of some high name. There was no difficulty in obtaining one from a British repository. The honorable gentleman has cited a speech of my Lord Goderich, (11) addressed to the British Parliament, in favor of free trade, and full of deep regret that old England *could not possibly* conform her practice of rigorous restriction and exclusion to her liberal *doctrines of* unfettered commerce, so earnestly recommended to foreign powers. Sir, [said Mr. C.] I know my Lord Goderich very well, although my acquaintance with him was prior to his being summoned to the British House of Peers. We both signed the convention between the United States and Great Britain of 1815.

He is an honorable man, frank, possessing business, but ordinary talents, about the stature and complexion of the honorable gentleman from South Carolina, a few years older than he, and every drop of blood running in his veins being pure and unadulterated Anglo-Saxon blood. If he were to live to the age of Methuselah, he could not make a speech of such ability and eloquence as that which the gentleman from South Carolina recently delivered to the Senate; and there would be much more fitness in my Lord Goderich making quotations from the speech of the gentleman, than his quoting, as authority, the theoretical doctrines of my Lord Goderich. We are too much in the habit of looking abroad, not merely for manufactured articles, but for the sanction of high names, to support favorite theories. I have seen, and closely observed, the British Parliament, and without derogating from its justly elevated character, I have no hesitation in saying, that in all the attributes of order, dignity, patriotism, and eloquence, the American Congress would not suffer, in the smallest degree, by a comparison with it.

I dislike this resort to authority, and especially *foreign and interested au*thority, for the support of principles of public policy. I would greatly prefer to meet gentlemen upon the broad ground of fact, of experience, and of reason; but, since they will appeal to British names and authority, I feel myself compelled to imitate their bad example. Allow me to quote from the speech of a member of the British Parliament, bearing the same family name with my Lord Goderich, but whether or not a relation of his, I do not know. The member alluded to was arguing against the violation of the treaty of Methuen—that treaty, not *less fa*tal to the interests of Portugal than would be the system of gentlemen to the best interests of America—and he went on to say:

It was idle for us to endeavor to persuade other nations to join with us in adopting the principles of what was called 'free trade.' Other nations knew, as well as the noble lord opposite, and those who acted with him, what we meant by 'free trade', was nothing more nor less than, by means of the great advantages we enjoyed, to get a monopoly of all their markets for our manufactures, and to prevent them, one and all, from ever becoming manufacturing nations.

When the system of reciprocity and free trade had been proposed to a French ambassador, his remark was, that the plan was excellent in theory, but, to make it fair in practice, it would be necessary to defer the attempt to put it in execution for half a century, until France should be on the same footing with Great Britain, in marine, in manufactures, in capital, and the many other peculiar advantages which it now enjoyed. The policy that France acted on, was that of encouraging its native manufactures, and it was a wise policy; because, if it were freely to admit our manufactures, it would speedily be reduced to the rank of an agricultural nation; and therefore a poor nation, as all must be that depend exclusively upon agriculture. America acted, too, upon the same principle with France. America legislated for futurity-legislated for an increasing population. America, too, was prosperous under this system. In twenty years, America would be independent of England for manufactures altogether...

But since the peace, France, Germany, America, and all the other countries of the world, had proceeded upon the principle of encouraging and protecting native manufactures.

But I have said that the system nominally called "free trade," so earnestly and eloquently recommended to our adoption, is a mere revival of the British colonial system, forced upon us by Great Britain during the existence of our colonial vassalage. The whole system is fully explained and illustrated in a work published as far back as the year 1750, entitled "The trade and navigation of Great Britain considered by Joshua Gee," with extracts from which I have been furnished by the diligent researches of a friend. It will be seen from these, that the South Carolina policy now, is identical with the long-cherished policy of Great Britain, which remains the same as it was when the thirteen colonies were part of the British Empire. In that work, the author contends—

1. That manufactures, In the American colonies, should be discouraged or prohibited.

Great Britain, with its dependencies, is doubtless as well able to subsist within itself as any nation in Europe. We have an enterprising people, fit for all the arts of peace and war. We have provisions in abundance, and those of the best sort, and are able to raise sufficient for double the number of inhabitants. We have the very best materials for clothing, and want nothing, either for use or even for luxury, but what we have at home, or might have from our colonies; so that we might make such an intercourse of trade among ourselves, or between us and them, as would maintain a vast navigation. But we ought always to keep a watchful eye over our colonies, to restrain them from setting up any of the manufactures which are carried on in Britain; and any such attempts should be crushed in the beginning; for if they are suffered to grow up to maturity, it will be difficult to suppress them.

Our colonies are much in the same state Ireland was in, when they began the woollen manufactory, and, as their numbers increased, will fall upon manufactures for clothing themselves, if due care be not taken to find employment for them in raising such productions as may enable them to furnish themselves with all their necessaries from us.

Then it was the object of this British economist to

adapt the means or wealth of the colonists to the *supply re*quired by their necessities, and to make the mother country the only source of that supply. Now it seems the policy is only so far to be reversed, that we must continue to import *necessaries fr*om Great Britain, in order to *enable he*r to purchase raw cotton from us.

I should, therefore, think it worthy the care of the Government to endeavor, by all possible means, to encourage them in raising of silk, hemp, flax, iron, [only pig, to be hammered in England,] pot ash, etc., by giving them competent bounties in the beginning, and sending over judicious and skillful persons, at the public charge, to assist and instruct them in the most proper methods of management, which, in my apprehension, would lay a foundation for establishing the most profitable trade of any we have. And considering the commanding situation of our colonies along the seacoast; the great convenience of navigable rivers in all of them; the cheapness of land, and the easiness of raising provisions; great numbers of people would transport themselves thither to settle upon such improvements. Now as people have been filled with fears that the colonies, if encouraged to raise rough materials, would set up for themselves, a little regulation would remove all those jealousies out of the way. They have never thrown or wove any silk as yet that we have heard of; therefore, if a law was made to prohibit the use of every throwster's mill, or doubling or horsling silk with any machine whatever, they would then send it us raw, and, as they will have the providing rough materials to themselves, so shall we have the manufacturing of them. If encouragement be given for raising hemp, flax, etc. doubtless they will soon begin to manufacture, if not prevented; therefore, to stop the progress of any such manufacture, it is proposed that no weaver there shall have liberty to set up any looms without first registering, at an office kept for that purpose, the name and place of abode of any journeyman that shall work with him. But if any particular inhabitant shall be inclined to have any linen or woolen made of their own spinning, they should not be abridged of the same liberty that they now make use of, viz, to carry to a weaver (who shall be licensed by the Governor) and have it wrought up for the use of the family, but not to be sold to any person in a private manner, nor exposed to any market or fair, upon pain of forfeiture. And, inasmuch as they have been supplied with all their iron manufactures from hence, except what is used in the building of ships and other country work, one-half of our exports being supposed to be in nails- a manufacture which they allow has never hitherto been carried on among them-it is proposed they shall, for time to come, never erect the manufacture of any under the size of a two shilling nail, horse nails, excepted; that all slitting mills, and engines for drawing wire, or weaving stockings be put down; and that every smith who keeps a common forge or shop, shall register his name and place of abode, and the name of every servant which he shall employ, which license shall be renewed once every year, and pay for the liberty of working at such trade. That all negroes shall be prohibited from weaving either linen or woollen, or spinning or combing of wool, or working at any manufacture of iron, further than making it into pig or bar iron. That they also be prohibited from manufacturing hats, stockings, or leather, of any kind. This limitation will not abridge the planters of any privilege they now enjoy. On the contrary, it will turn their industry to promoting and raising those rough materials.

The author then proposes that the Board of Trade and Plantations should be furnished with statistical accounts of the various *permitted manufactures*, to enable them to encourage or repress the industry of the colonists, and prevent the danger of interference with British industry.

It is hoped that this method would allay the heat that some people have shown for destroying the iron works on the plantations, and pulling down all their forges; taking away, in a violent manner, their estates and properties; preventing the husbandmen from getting their ploughshares, carts, and other utensils, mended; destroying the manufacture of ship building, by depriving them of the liberty of making bolts, spikes, and other things proper for carrying on that work; by which article, returns are made for purchasing our woollen manufactures.

Such is the picture of colonists dependent upon the mother country for their necessary supplies, drawn by a writer who was not among the number of those who desired to debar them the means of building a vessel, erecting a forge, or mending a ploughshare, but who was willing to promote their growth and property, as far as was consistent with the paramount interests of the manufacturing or parent state.

2. The advantages to Great Britain from keeping the colonies dependent on her for their essential supplies.

If we examine into the circumstances of the inhabitants of our plantations and our own, it will appear that not one-fourth part of their product redounds to their own profit; for out of all that comes here, they only carry back clothing and other accommodations for their families; all of which is of the merchandise and manufacture of this kingdom.

After showing how this system tends to concentrate all the surplus of acquisition over absolute expenditure, in England, he says:

All these advantages we receive by the plantations, besides the mortgages on the planters' estates, and the high interest they pay us, which is very considerable; and therefore very great care ought to be taken, in regulating all affairs of the colonists, that the planters be not put under too many difficulties, but encouraged to go on cheerfully.

New England and the northern colonies, have not commodities and products enough to send us in return for purchasing their necessary clothing, but are under very great difficulties; and, therefore, any ordinary sort sell with them. And when they have grown out of fashion with us, they are new fashioned enough there.

Sir, I cannot go on with this disgusting detail. Their refuse goods; their old shopkeepers; their cast-off clothes, good enough for us! Was there ever a scheme more artfully devised, by which the energies and faculties of one people should be kept down and rendered subservient to the pride, and the pomp, and the power of another! The system then proposed differs only from that which is now recommended, in one particular—that was intended to be enforced by power, this would not be less effectually executed by the force of circumstances. A gentleman in Boston, (Mr. Lee,) the agent of the free trade convention, from whose exhaustless mint there is a constant issue of reports, seems to envy the blessed condition of dependent Canada, when compared to the oppressed state of this Union; and it is a fair inference from the view which he presents, that he would have us to hasten back to the golden days of that colonial bondage, which is so well depicted in the work from which I have been quoting. Mr. Lee exhibits two tabular statements, in one of which he presents the high duties which he represents to be paid in the ports of the United States, and, in the other, those which are paid in Canada, generally about 2 percent ad valorem. But did it not occur to him that the duties levied in Canada are paid chiefly on British manufactures, or on articles passing from one to another part of a common empire; and that, to present a parallel case, in the United States, he ought to have shown that importations made into one state from another, which are now free, are subject to the same or higher duties than are paid in Canada?

False Arguments Refuted

I will now, Mr. President, proceed to a more particular consideration of the arguments urged against the protective system, and an inquiry into its practical operation, especially on the cotton-growing country, And, as I wish to state and meet the argument fairly, I invite correction of my statement of it, if necessary. It is alleged that the system operates prejudicially to the cotton to the cotton planter, by diminishing the foreign demands for his staple; that we cannot sell to Great Britain, unless we buy from her; that the import duty is equivalent to an export duty, and falls upon the cotton grower; that South Carolina pays a disproportionate quota of the public revenue; that an abandonment of the protective policy would lead to an augmentation of our exports of an amount not less than one hundred and fifty millions of dollars; and, finally, that the South cannot partake of the advantages of manufacturing, if there be any. Let us examine these various propositions, in detail.

1. That the foreign demand for cotton is diminished; and that we cannot sell to Great Britain unless we buy from her. The demand of both our great foreign customers is constantly and annually increasing. It is true that the ratio of the increase may not be equal to that of production; but this is owing to the fact that the power of producing the raw material is much greater, and is therefore constantly in the advance of the power of consumption. A single fact will illustrate. The average produce of laborers engaged in the cultivation of cotton may be estimated at five bales, or fifteen hundred weight to the hand. Supposing the annual average consumption of each individual who uses cotton cloth to be five pounds, one hand can produce enough of the raw material to clothe three hundred.

The argument comprehends two errors, one of fact

and the other of principle. It assumes that we do not in fact purchase of Great Britain. What is the true state of the case? There are certain, but very few articles which it is thought sound policy requires that we should manufacture at home, and on these the tariff operates. But, with respect to all the rest, and much the larger number of articles of taste, fashion, or utility, they are subject to no other than revenue duties, and are freely introduced. I have before me, from the treasury, a statement of our imports from England, Scotland, and Ireland, including ten years preceding the last and three quarters of the last year, from which it will appear that, although there are some fluctuations in the amount of the different years, the largest amount imported in any one year has been since the tariff of 1824, and that the last year's importation, when the returns of the fourth quarter shall be received, will probably be the greatest in the whole term of eleven years.

Now, if it be admitted that there is a less amount of the protected articles imported from Great Britain, she may be, and probably is, compensated for the deficiency by the increased consumption in America of the articles of her industry not falling within the scope of the policy of our protection. The establishment of manufactures among us excites the creation of wealth, and this gives new powers of consumption, which are gratified by the purchase of foreign objects. A poor nation can never be a great consuming nation. Its poverty will limit its consumption to bare subsistence.

The erroneous principle which the argument includes, is, that it devolves on us the duty of taking care that Great Britain shall be enabled to purchase from us, without exacting from Great Britain the corresponding duty. If it be true, on one side, that nations are bound to shape their policy in reference to the ability of foreign powers, it must be true on both sides of the Atlantic. And this reciprocal obligation ought to be emphatically regarded towards the nation supplying the raw material, by the manufacturing nation, because the industry of the latter gives four or five values to what had been produced by the industry of the former.

But, does Great Britain practise towards us upon the principles which we are now required to observe in regard to her? The exports to the United Kingdom, as appears from the same treasury statement just adverted to, during eleven years, from 1821 to 1831, and exclusive of the fourth quarter of the last year, fall short of the amount of imports by upwards of $46 million, and the total amount, when the returns of that quarter are received, will exceed $50 million! It is surprising how we have been able to sustain, for so long a time, a trade so very unequal. We must have been absolutely ruined by it, if the unfavorable balance had not been neutralized by more profitable commerce with other parts of the world. Of all nations Great Britain has the least cause to complain of the trade between the two countries. Our imports from that single power are nearly one-third of the entire amount of our importations from all foreign countries together. Great Britain constantly acts on the maxim of buying only what she wants and cannot produce, and selling to foreign nations the utmost amount she can. In conformity with this maxim, she excludes articles of prime necessity produced by us— equally if not more necessary than any of her industry which we tax, although the admission of those articles would increase our ability to purchase from her, according to the argument of gentlemen.

If we purchased still less from Great Britain than we do, and our conditions were reversed, so that the value of her imports from this country exceeded that of her exports to it, she would only then be compelled to do what we have so long done, and what South Carolina does, in her trade with Kentucky—make up for the unfavorable balance by trade with other places and countries. How does she now dispose of the $160 millions worth of cotton fabrics, which she annually sells? Of that amount the United States do not purchase 5 percent. What becomes of the other 95 percent? Is it not sold to other powers, and would not their markets remain if ours were totally shut? Would she not continue, as she now finds it her interest, to purchase the raw material from us, to supply those markets? Would she be guilty of the folly of depriving herself of markets to the amount of upwards of $150 millions, because we refused her a market for some $8 or $10 millions?

But if there were a diminution of the British demand for cotton, equal to the loss of a market for the few British fabrics which are within the scope of our protective policy, the question would still remain, whether the cotton planter is not amply indemnified by the creation of additional demand elsewhere. With respect to the cotton grower, it is the *totality of* the demand, and not its *distribution*, which affects his interests. If any system of policy will augment the aggregate of the demand, that system is favorable to his interests, although its tendency may be to vary the theatre of the demand. It could not, for example, be injurious to him, if, instead of Great Britain continuing to receive the entire quantity of cotton which she now does, 200 or 300 thousand bales of it were taken to the other side of the channel, and increased, to that extent, the French demand. It would be better for him, because it is always better to have several markets than one. Now, if, instead of a transfer to the opposite side of the channel of those 200 or 300 thousand bales, they are transported to the northern states, can that be injurious to the cotton grower? Is it not better for him? Is it not better to have a market at home, unaffected by war or other foreign causes, for that amount of his staple?

If the establishment of American manufactures, therefore, had the sole effect of creating a new, and an American, demand for cotton, *exactly to* the same extent in which it lessened the British demand, there would be no just cause of complaint against the tariff. The gain in one place would precisely equal the loss in the other. But the true state of the matter is much more favorable to the cotton grower. It is calculated that the cotton manufactories of the United States absorb at least 200 thousand bales of cotton annually. I believe it to be more. The two ports of Boston and Providence alone received, during the last year, near 110 thousand bales. The amount is annually increasing. The raw material of that 200 thousand bales is worth $6 millions, and there is an additional value conferred by the manufacturer, of $18 millions; it being generally calculated that, in such cotton fabrics as we are in the habit of making, the manufacture constitutes three-fourths of the value of the article. If, therefore, these $24 millions worth of cotton fabrics were not made in the United States, but were manufactured in Great Britain, in order to obtain them, we should have to add to the already enormous disproportion between the amount of our imports and exports, in the trade with Great Britain, the further sum of $24 millions, or, deducting the price of the raw material, $18 millions! And will gentlemen tell me how it would be possible for this country to sustain such a ruinous trade? From all that portion of the United States lying north and east of James River, and west of the mountains, Great Britain receives comparatively nothing. How would it be possible for the inhabitants of that largest portion of our territory to supply themselves with cotton fabrics, if they were brought from England exclusively? They could not do it. But for the existence of the American manufacture, they would be compelled greatly to curtail their supplies, if not absolutely to suffer in their comforts. By its existence at home, the circle of those exchanges is created, which reciprocally diffuses among all who are embraced within it the productions of their respective industry. The cotton grower sells the raw material to the manufacturer; he buys the iron, the bread, the meal, the coal, and the countless number of objects of his consumption, from his fellow-citizens, and they, in turn, purchase his fabrics. Putting it upon the ground merely of supplying those with necessary articles, who could not otherwise obtain them, ought there to be, from any quarter, an objection to the only system by which that object can be accomplished? But can there be any doubt, with those who will reflect, that the actual amount of cotton consumed is increased by the home manufacture? The main argument of gentlemen is founded upon the idea of mutual ability resulting from mutual exchanges. *They would* furnish an ability to foreign nations by purchasing from them, and I to our own people, by exchanges at home. If the American manufacture were discontinued, and that of England were to take its place, how would she sell the additional quantity of $24 millions of cotton goods which we now cake? To us? That has been shown to be impracticable. To other foreign nations? She has already pushed her supplies to them to the utmost extent. The ultimate consequence would, then, be to diminish the total consumption of cotton, to say nothing now of the reduction of price that would take place by throwing into the ports of Great Britain the 200 thousand bales which, no longer being manufactured in the United States, would go thither.

2. That the import duty is equivalent to an export duty, and falls on the producer of cotton.

[Here Mr. HAYNE explained, and said that he never contended that an import duty was equivalent to an export duty, under all circumstances, he had explained in his speech his ideas of the precise operation of the existing system. To which Mr. CLAY replied that he had seen the argument so stated in some of the ingenious essays from the South Carolina press, and would therefore answer it.]

The framers of our Constitution, by granting the

power to Congress to lay import, and prohibiting that of laying an export duty, manifested that they did not regard them as equivalent. Nor does the common sense of mankind. An export fastens upon, and incorporates itself with, the article on which it is laid. The article cannot escape from it—it pursues and follows it wherever the article goes; and if, in the foreign market, the supply is above or just equal to the demand, the amount of the export duty will be a clear deduction to the exporter from the price of the article. But an import duty on a foreign article leaves the exporter of the domestic article free, 1st, to import specie; 2nd, goods which are free from the protecting duty; or, 3rd, such goods as, being chargeable with the protecting duty, he can sell at home, and throw the duty on the consumer.

But it is confidently argued that the import duty falls upon the grower of cotton; and the case has been put in debate, and again and again, in conversation, of the South Carolina planter, who exports 100 bales of cotton to Liverpool, exchanges them for 100 bales of merchandise, and, when he brings them home, being compelled to leave at the customhouse 40 bales in the form of duties. The argument is founded on the assumption that a duty of 40 percent amounts to a subtraction of 40 from the 100 bales of merchandise. The first objection to it is, that it supposes a case of barter which never occurs. If it be replied that it, nevertheless, occurs in the operations of commerce, the answer would be, that, since the export of Carolina cotton is chiefly made by New York or foreign merchants, the loss stated, if it really accrued, would fall upon them, and not upon the planter. But, to test the correctness of the hypothetical case, let us suppose that the duty, instead of 40 percent, should be 150, which is asserted to be the duty in some cases. Then, the planter would not only lose the whole 100 bales of merchandise which he had gotten for his 100 bales of cotton, but he would have to purchase with other means, and additional 50 bales, in order to enable him to pay the duties accruing on the proceeds of the cotton. Another answer is, that if the *producer of* cotton in America, exchanged against English fabrics, pays the duty, the *producer of* those fabrics also pays it, and then it is twice paid. Such must be the consequence, unless the principle is true on one side of the Atlantic, and false on the other. The true answer is, that the exporter of an article, if he invests its proceeds in a foreign market, takes care to make the investment in such merchandise as, when brought home, he can sell with a fair profit; and, consequently, the consumer would pay the original cost and charges and profit.

3. The next objection to the American System is, that it subjects South Carolina to the payment of an undue proportion of the public revenue. The basis of this

objection is the assumption, shown to have been erroneous, that the producer of the exports from this country pays the duty on its imports, instead of the consumer of those imports. The amount which South Carolina really contributes to the public revenue, no more than that of any other state, can be precisely ascertained. It depends upon her consumption of articles paying duties, and we may make an approximation sufficient for all practical purposes. The cotton planters of the valley of the Mississippi, with which I am acquainted, generally expend about one-third of their income in the support of their families and plantations. On this subject, I hold in my hands a statement from a friend of mine, of great accuracy, and a member of the Senate. According to this statement, in a crop of $10 thousand, the expenses may fluctuate between $2,800, and $3,200. Of this sum, about one-fourth, from $700 to $800, may be laid out in articles paying the protecting duty; the residue is disbursed for provisions, mules, horses, oxen, wages of overseer, etc. Estimating the exports of South Carolina at $8 millions, one-third is $2,666,666; of which, one-fourth will be $666,666.66. Now supposing the protecting duty to be 50 percent, and that it all enters into the price of the article, the amount paid by South Carolina would only be $333,333.33. But the total revenue of the United States may be stated at $25 millions, of which, the proportion of South Carolina, whatever standard, whether of wealth or population, be adopted, would be about $1 million. Of course, on this view of the subject, she actually pays only about one-third of her fair and legitimate share. I repeat, that I have no personal knowledge of the habits of actual expenditure in South Carolina; they may be greater than I have stated, in respect to other parts of the cotton country, but, if they are, that fact does not arise from any defect in the system of public policy.

4. An abandonment of the American System it is urged, would lead to an addition to our exports of $150 millions. The amount of $150 millions of cotton, in the raw state, would $450 millions in the manufactured state, supposing no greater measure of value be communicated, in the manufactured form, than that which our industry imparts. Now, sir, where would markets be found for this vast addition to the supply? Not in the United States, certainly, nor in any other quarter of the globe, England having already everywhere pressed her cotton manufactures to the utmost point of repletion. We must look out for new worlds, seek from new and unknown races of mortals, to consume this immense increase of cotton fabrics.

[Mr. HAYNE said that he did not mean that the increase of $150 millions to the amount of our exports, would be of cotton alone, but of other articles.]

What *other articles?* Agricultural produce-breadstuffs-
beef and pork? Etc. *Where* s*h*all we find markets for
them? *Whither* s*h*all we go? To *what country*, whose
ports are not hermetically sealed against their
admission? Break down the home market, and you
are without resource. Destroy all other interests in the
country, for the imaginary purpose of advancing the
cotton planting interest, and you inflict a positive
injury, without the smallest practical benefit to the
cotton planter. Could Charleston, or the whole South,
when all other markets are prostrated, or shut against
the reception of the surplus of our farmers, receive
that surplus? Would they buy more than they might
want for their own consumption? Could they find
markets which other parts of the Union could not?
Would gentlemen *force the* freemen of all north of
James River, east and west, like the miserable slave,
on the Sabbath day, to repair to Charleston, with a
turkey under his arm, or a pack upon his back, and
beg the clerk of some English or Scotch merchant,
living in his gorgeous palace, or rolling in his
splendid coach in the streets, to exchange his *"truck"*
for a bit of flannel to cover his naked wife and
children! No! I am sure that I do no more than justice
to their hearts, when I believe that they would reject
what I believe to be the inevitable effects of their
policy.
5. But it is contended, in the last place, that the South

cannot, from physical and other causes, engage in the manufacturing arts. I deny the premises, and I deny the conclusion. I deny the fact of inability, and, if it existed, I deny the conclusion that we must, therefore, break down our manufactures, and nourish those of foreign countries. The South possesses, in an extraordinary degree, two of the most important elements of manufacturing industry—water power and labor. The former gives to our whole country a most decided advantage over Great Britain. But a single experiment, stated by the gentleman from South Carolina, in which a faithless slave put the torch to a manufacturing establishment, has discouraged similar enterprises. We have, in Kentucky, the same description of population, and we employ them, and almost exclusively employ them, in many of our hemp manufactories. A neighbor of mine, one of our most opulent and respectable citizens, has had one, two, if not three, manufactories burnt by incendiaries; but he persevered, and his perseverance has been rewarded with wealth. We found that it was less expensive to keep night watches, than to pay premiums for insurance, and we employed them.

Let it be supposed, however, that the South cannot manufacture; must those parts of the Union which *can*, be therefore prevented? Must we support those of foreign countries? I am sure that injustice would be done to the generous and patriotic nature of South Carolina, if it were believed that she envied or repined at the success of other portions of the Union in branches of industry to which she might happen not to be adapted. Through her whole career she has been liberal, national, high-minded.

The friends of the American System have been reminded, by the honorable gentleman from Maryland [Mr. Smith], (12) that they are the majority, and he has admonished them to exercise their power in moderation. The *majority ou*ght never to trample upon the feelings, or violate the just rights of the minority. They ought never to triumph over the fallen, nor to make any but a temperate and equitable use of their power. But these counsels come with an ill grace from the gentleman from Maryland. He too, is a member of a *majority—a* political majority. And how has the administration of that majority exercised their power in this country? Recall to your recollection the 4th of March, 1829, when the lank, lean, famished forms, from fen and forest, and the four quarters of the Union, gathered together in the halls of patronage, or stealing, by evening's twilight, into the apartments of the president's mansion, cried out, with ghastly faces, and in sepulchral tones, Give us bread! Give us treasury pap! Give us our reward! England's bard was mistaken, ghosts will sometimes come, called or uncalled. Go to the families who were driven from the employments on which they were dependent for subsistence, in consequence of their exercise of the dearest right of freemen. Go to mothers, whilst hugging to their bosoms their starving children. Go to fathers, who, after being disqualified, by long public service, for any other business, were stripped of their humble places, and then sought, by the minions of authority, to be stripped of all that was left them—their good names—and ask, what mercy was shown to them! As for myself, born in the midst of the revolution, the first air that I ever breathed on my native soil of Virginia having been that of liberty and independence, I never expected justice nor desired mercy at their hands; and scorn the wrath, and defy the oppression of power!

I regret, Mr. President, that one topic has, I think unnecessarily, been introduced into this debate. I allude to the charge brought against the manufacturing system, as favoring the growth of aristocracy. If it were true, would gentlemen prefer supporting foreign accumulations of wealth, by that description of industry, rather than their own country? But is it correct? The joint stock companies of the North, as I understand them, are nothing more than associations, sometimes of hundreds, by means of which the small earnings of many are brought into a common stock; and the associates, obtaining corporate privileges, are enabled to prosecute, under one superintending head, their business to better advantage. Nothing can be more essentially democratic, or better devised to counterpoise the influence of individual wealth. In Kentucky, almost every manufactory known to me is in the hands of enterprising self-made men, who have acquired whatever wealth they possess by patient and diligent labor. Comparisons are odious, and, but in defence, would not be made by me. But is there more tendency to aristocracy in a manufactory, supporting hundreds of freemen, or in a cotton plantation, with its not less numerous slaves, sustaining, perhaps, only two white families—that of the master and the overseer?

Cheaper and Better Items

I pass with pleasure, from this disagreeable topic to two general proposition which cover the entire ground of debate. The first is, that, under the operation of the American System, the objects which it protects and fosters are brought to the consumer at cheaper prices than they commanded prior to its introduction, or than they would command if it did not exist. If that be true, ought not the country to be contented and satisfied with the system, unless the second proposition, which I mean presently also to consider, is unfounded? And that is, that the tendency of the system is to sustain, and that it has upheld the prices of all our agricultural and other produce, including cotton.

And is the fact not indisputable, that all essential objects of consumption, affected by the tariff, are cheaper and better, since the act of 1824, than they were for several years prior to that law? I appeal, for its truth, to common observation and to all practical men. I appeal to the farmer of the country, whether he does not purchase, on better terms, his iron, salt, brown sugar, cotton goods, and woollens, for his laboring people. And I ask the cotton planter if he has not been better and more cheaply supplied with his cotton bagging. In regard to this latter article, the gentleman from South Carolina was mistaken in supposing that I complained that, under the existing duty, the Kentucky manufacturer could not compete with the Scotch. The Kentuckian furnishes a more substantial and a cheaper article, and at a more uniform and regular price. But it was the frauds, the violations of law, of which I did complain; not smuggling, in the common sense of that practice, which as something bold, daring, and enterprising in it, but mean, bare-faced cheating by fraudulent invoices and false denomination.

I plant myself upon this FACT of cheapness and superiority, as upon impregnable ground. Gentlemen may tax their ingenuity, and produce a thousand speculative solutions of the fact but the fact itself will remain undisturbed. Let us look into some particulars. The total consumption of bar iron in the United States is supposed to be about 146,000 tons, of which 112,866 tons are made within the country, and the residue imported. The number of men employed in the manufacture is estimated at 29,254, and the total number of persons subsisted by it at 146,273. The measure of protection extended to this necessary article was never fully adequate until the passage of the act of 1828; and what has been the consequence? The annual increase of quantity, since that period, has been in a ratio of near 25 percent, and the wholesale price of bar iron in the northern cities was, in 1828, $105 per ton; in 1829, $100; in 1830, $90; and in 1831, from $85 to $75—constantly diminishing. We import very little English iron, and that which we do is very inferior, and only adapted to a few purposes. In instituting a comparison between that inferior article and our superior iron, subjects, entirely different, are compared. They are made by different processes. The English cannot make iron of equal quality to ours, at a less price than we do. They have three classes, best-best, and best, and ordinary. It is the latter which is imported. Of the whole amount imported, there is only about four thousand tons of foreign iron that pays the high duty; the residue paying only a duty of about 30 percent, estimated on the prices of the importation of 1829. Our iron ore is superior to that of Great Britain, yielding often from 60 to 80 percent whilst theirs produces only about 25. This fact is so well known, that I have heard of recent exportations of iron ore to England.

It has been alleged that bar iron, being a raw material, ought to be admitted free, or with low duties, for the sake of the manufacturers themselves. But I take this to be the true principle, that, if our country is producing a raw material of prime necessity, and, with reasonable protection, can produce it in sufficient quantity to supply our wants, that raw material ought to be protected, although it may be proper to protect the article also out of which it is manufactured. The tailor will ask protection for himself, but wishes it denied to the grower of wool and the manufacturer of broadcloth. The cotton planter enjoys protection for the raw material, but does not desire it to be extended to the cotton manufacturer. The shipbuilder will ask protection for navigation, but does not wish it extended to the essential articles which enter into the construction of his ship. Each, in his proper vocation, solicits protection, but would have it denied to all other interests which are supposed to come into collision with his. Now, the duty of the statesman is, to elevate himself above these petty conflicts; calmly to survey all the various interests, and deliberately to proportion the measure of protection to each, according to its nature and to the general wants of society. It is quite possible that, in the degree of protection which has been afforded to the various workers in iron, there may be some error committed, although I have lately read an argument of much ability, proving that no injustice has really been done to them. If there be, it ought to be remedied.

The next article to which I would call the attention of the Senate, is that of cotton fabrics. The success of our manufacture of coarse cottons is generally admitted. It is demonstrated by the fact that they meet the cotton fabrics of other countries in foreign markets, and maintain a successful competition with them. There has been a gradual increase of the export of this article, which is sent to Mexico and the South American republics, to the Mediterranean, and even to Asia. The remarkable fact was lately communicated to me, that the *same individual* who, twenty-five years ago, was engaged in the importation of cotton cloth from Asia, for American consumption, is now engaged in the exportation of coarse American cottons to Asia, for Asiatic consumption! And my honorable friend from Massachusetts, now in my eye, [Mr. SILSBEE] (13) informed me that, on his departure from home, among the last orders which he gave, one was for the exportation of coarse cottons to Sumatra, in the vicinity of Calcutta! I hold in my hand a statement, derived from the most authentic source, showing the *identical de*scription of cotton cloth, which sold, in 1817, at 29 cents per yard, was sold, in 1819, at 21 cents; in 1821, at 19 1/2 cents; in 1823, at 17 cents; and in 1825, at 14 1/2 cents; in 1827, at 13 cents; in 1829, at 9 cents; in 1830, at 9 1/2 cents; and in 1831, at from 10 1/2 to 11. Such is the wonderful effect of protection, competition, and improvement in skill, combined! The year 1829 was one of some suffering to this branch of industry, probably owing to the principle of competition being pushed too far; and hence we observe a small rise in the article the next two years. The introduction of the calico printing into the United States constitutes an important era in our manufacturing industry. It commenced about the year 1825, and has since made such astonishing advances, that the whole quantity now annually printed is but little short of forty millions of yards—about two-thirds of our whole consumption. It is a beautiful manufacture, combining great mechanical skill with scientific discoveries in chemistry. The engraved cylinders for making the impression require much taste, and put in requisition the genius of the fine arts of design and engraving. Are the fine graceful forms of our fair countrywomen less lovely when enveloped in the chintzes and calicoes produced by native industry, than when clothed in the tinsel of foreign drapery?

Gentlemen are, no doubt, surprised at these facts. They should not underrate the energies, the enterprise, and the skill of our fellow-citizens. I have no doubt they are every way competent to accomplish whatever can be effected by any other people, if encouraged and protected by the fostering care of our own government. Will gentlemen believe the fact, which I am authorized now to state, that the United States, at this time, manufacture one half the quantity of cotton which Great Britain did in 1816! We possess three great advantages: First. The raw material. Second. Water power instead of that of steam, generally used in England. And third. The cheaper labor of females. In England, males spin with the mule and weave; in this country, women and girls spin with the throstle, and superintend the power loom. And can there be any employment more appropriate? Who has not been delighted with contemplating the clock-work regularity of a large cotton manufactory? I have often visited them, at Cincinnati and other places, and always with increased admiration. The women, separated from the other sex, work in apartments, large, airy, well warmed, and spacious. Neatly dressed, with ruddy complexions, and happy countenances, they watch the work before them, mend the broken threads, and replace the exhausted balls or broaches. At stated hours they are called to their meals, and go and return with light and cheerful step. At night they separate, and repair to their respective houses, under the care of a mother, guardian, or friend. "Six days shalt thou labor and do all that thou hast to do, but the seventh day is the Sabbath of the Lord thy God." Accordingly, we behold them, on that sacred day, assembled together in His temples, and in devotional attitudes and with pious countenances, offering their prayers to Heaven for all its blessings. Of which it is not the least that a system of policy has been adopted by their country, which admits of their obtaining comfortable subsistence. Manufacturers have brought into profitable employment a vast amount of female labor, which, without them, would be lost to the country.

In respect to woollens, every gentleman's own observation and experience will enable him to judge of the great reduction of price which has taken place in most of these articles since the tariff of 1824. It would have been still greater, but for the high duty on the raw material imposed for the particular benefit of the farming interest. But, without going into particular details, I shall limit myself to inviting the attention of the Senate to a single article of general and necessary use. The protection given to flannels in

1828 was fully adequate. It has enabled the American manufacturer to obtain complete possession of the American market; and now let us look at the effect. I have before me a statement from a highly respectable mercantile house, showing the price of four descriptions of flannel, during six years. The average price of them, in 1826, 38 3/4 cents; in 1827, 38; in 1828, (the year of the tariff) 46; in 1829, 36; in 1830, (notwithstanding the advance in the price of wool) 32; and in 1831, 32 1/4. These facts require no comments. I have before me another statement, of a practical and respectable man, well versed in the flannel manufacture in America and England. demonstrating that the cost of manufacture is precisely the same in both countries; and that, although a yard of flannel, which would sell in England at 15 cents, would command here 22, the difference of 7 cents is the exact difference between the cost in the two countries of the six ounces of wool contained in a yard of flannel.

Brown sugar, during ten years, from 1792 to 1802, with a duty of 1 1/2 cents per pound, averaged 14 cents per pound. The same article during ten years, from 1820 to 1830, with a duty of 3 cents, has averaged only 8 cents per pound. Nails, with a duty of 5 cents per pound are selling at 6 cents. Window glass, eight by ten, prior to the tariff of 1824, sold at $12 or $13 per hundred feet; it now sells for $3.75.

The gentleman from South Carolina, sensible of the

incontestable fact of the very great reduction in the prices of the necessaries of life, protected by the American System, has felt the full force of it, and has presented various explanations of the causes to which he ascribes it. The first is the diminished production of the precious metals, in consequence of the distressed state of the countries in which they are extracted, and the consequent increase of their value relative to that of the commodities for which they are exchanged. But if this be the true cause of the reduction of price, its operation ought to have been general on all objects, and of course upon cotton among the rest. And, in point of fact, the diminished price of that staple is not greater than the diminution of the value of other staples of our agriculture. Flour, which commanded, some years ago, $10 or $12 per barrel, is now sold for five. The fall of tobacco has been still more. The Kitefoot of Maryland, which sold at from $16 to $20 per hundred, now produces only $4 or $5. That of Virginia has sustained an equal decline. Beef, pork, every article, almost, produced by the farmer has decreased in value. Ought not South Carolina then to submit quietly to a state of things which is general, and proceeds from an uncontrollable cause? Ought she to ascribe to the "accursed" tariff what results from the calamities of civil and foreign war, raging in many countries?

But, sir, I do not subscribe to this doctrine implicitly. I

do not believe that the diminished production of the precious metals, if that be the fact, satisfactorily accounts for the fall in prices. For I think that the augmentation of the currency of the world, by means of banks, public stocks, and other facilities arising out of exchange and credit, has more than supplied any deficiency in the amount of the precious metals.

It is further urged that the restoration of peace in Europe, after the battle of Waterloo, and the consequent return to peaceful pursuits of large masses of its population, by greatly increasing the aggregate amount of effective labor, had a tendency to lower prices; and undoubtedly such ought to have been its natural tendency. The same cause, however, must also have operated to reduce the price of our agricultural produce, for which there was no longer the same demand in peace as in war—and it did so operate. But its influence on the price of manufactured articles, between the general peace of Europe in 1815, and the adoption of our tariff in 1824, was less sensibly felt, because perhaps a much larger portion of the labor, liberated by the disbandment of armies, was absorbed by manufactures than by agriculture. It is also contended that the invention and improvement of labor-saving machinery have tended to lessen the prices of manufactured objects of consumption; and undoubtedly this cause has had some effect. Ought not America to contribute her quota of this cause, and has she not, by her skill and extraordinary adaptation to the arts, in truth, largely contributed to it?

Benefits of Competition

This brings me to consider what I apprehend to have been the most efficient of all the causes in the reduction of the prices of manufactured articles; and that is, COMPETITION. By competition, the total amount of the supply is increased, and by increase of the supply a competition in the sale ensues, and this enables the consumer to buy at lower rates. Of all human powers operating on the affairs of mankind, none is greater than that of competition. It is action and reaction. It operates between individuals in the same nation, and between different nations. It resembles the meeting of the mountain torrent, grooving, by its precipitous motion, its own channel, and ocean's tide. Unopposed, it sweeps everything before it; but, counterpoised, the waters become calm, safe, and regular. It is like the segments of a circle or an arch; taken separately, each is nothing; but, in their combination, they produce efficiency, symmetry, and perfection. By the American System this vast power has been excited in America, and brought into being to act in cooperation or collision with European industry. Europe acts within itself, and with America; and America acts within itself, and with Europe. The consequence is the reduction of prices in both hemispheres. Nor is it fair to argue, from the reduction of prices in Europe, to her own presumed skill and labor, exclusively. We affect her prices, and she affects ours. This must always be the case, at least in reference to any articles as to which there is not a total nonintercourse; and if our industry, by diminishing the demand for her supplies, should produce a diminution in the price of those supplies, it would be very unfair to ascribe that reduction to her ingenuity, instead of placing it to the credit of our own skill and excited industry.

Practical men understand very well this state of the case, whether they do or do not comprehend the causes which produce it. I have in my possession a letter from a respectable merchant, well known to me, in which he says, after complaining of the operation of the tariff of 1828 on the articles to which it applies, some of which he had imported, and that his purchases having been made in England before the passage of that tariff was known, it produced such an effect upon the English market, that the articles could not be resold without loss; he adds: "for *really it* appears that, when additional duties are laid upon an article, it then becomes *lower in*stead of *higher."* This could not probably happen where the supply of the foreign article did not exceed the home demand, unless upon the supposition of the increased duty having *excited or stimulated th*e measure of the home production.

The great law of *price is* determined by supply and demand. Whatever affects either, affects the price. If the supply is increased, the demand remaining the same, the price declines; if the demand is increased, the supply remaining the same, the price advances; if both supply and demand are undiminished, the price is stationary, and the price is influenced exactly in proportion to the degree of disturbance to the demand or supply. It is therefore a great error to suppose that an existing or new duty *necessarily be*comes a component element, to its exact amount, of price. If the proportions of demand and supply are varied by the duty, either in augmenting the supply, or diminishing the demand, or vice versa, price is affected, to the extent of that variation. But the duty never becomes an integral part of the price, except in instances where the demand and the supply remain, after the duty is imposed, precisely what they were before, or the demand is increased, and the supply remains stationary.

Competition, therefore, wherever existing, whether at home or abroad, is the parent cause of cheapness. If a high duty excites production at home, and the quantity of the domestic article exceeds the amount which had been previously imported, the price will fall. This accounts for an extraordinary fact stated by a senator from Missouri. Three cents were laid as a duty upon a pound of lead, by the act of 1828. The price at Galena and the other lead mines afterwards fell to one and a half cents per pound. Now it is obvious that the duty did not, in this case, enter into the price: for it was twice the amount of the price. What produced the fall? It was *stimulated* production at home, exerted by the temptation of the exclusive possession of the home market. This state of things could not last. Men would not continue an unprofitable pursuit; some abandoned the business, or the total quantity produced was diminished, and living prices have been the consequence. But, break down the domestic supply; place us again in a state of dependence on the foreign source; and can it be doubted that we should, ultimately, have to supply ourselves at dearer rates? It is not fair to credit the foreign market with the depression of prices, produced there by the influence of our competition. Let the competition be withdrawn, and their prices would instantly rise. On this subject, great mistakes are committed. I have seen some most erroneous reasoning, in a late report of Mr. Lee, of the free trade convention, in regard to the article of sugar. He calculates the total amount of brown sugar produced in the world, and then states that what is made in Louisiana is not more than 2 1/2 percent of that total. Although his data may be questioned, let us assume their truth, and what might be the result? Price being determined by the proportions of supply and demand, it is evident that, when the supply *exceeds the* demand, the price will fall. And the fall is not always regulated by the amount of that excess. If the market, at a given price, required 5 or 50 millions of hogsheads of sugar, a surplus of only a few hundred might materially influence the price, and diffuse itself throughout the whole mass. Add therefore, the 80,000 or 100,000 hogsheads of Louisiana sugar to the entire mass produced in other parts of the world, and it cannot be doubted that a material reduction of the price of the article, throughout Europe and America, would take place. The Louisiana sugar substituting foreign sugar, in the home market, to the amount of its annual produce, would force an equal amount of foreign sugar into other markets, which being glutted, the price would necessarily decline, and this decline of price would press portions of the foreign sugar into competition, in the United States, with Louisiana sugar, the price of which would also be brought down. The fact has been in exact conformity with this theory. But now let us suppose the Louisiana sugar to be entirely withdrawn from the general consumption, what then would happen? A new demand would be created in America for foreign sugar, to the extent of the 80,000 or 100,000 hogsheads made in Louisiana; a less amount, by that quantity, would be sent to the European markets; and the price would, consequently, everywhere rise. It is not, therefore those who, by keeping on duties, keep down prices, that tax the people; but those who, by repealing duties, would raise prices, that really impose burdens upon the people.

But it is argued that if, by the skill, experience, and perfection which we have acquired in certain branches of manufacture, they can be made as cheap as similar articles abroad, and enter fairly into competition with them, why not repeal the duties as to those articles? And why should we? Assuming the truth of the supposition, the foreign article would not be introduced in a *regular* course of trade, but would remain excluded by the possession of the home market which the domestic article had obtained. The repeal, therefore, would have no legitimate effect. But, might not the foreign article be imported in vast quantities, to glut our markets, break down our establishments, and ultimately, to enable the foreigner to monopolize the supply of our consumption? America is the greatest foreign market for European manufactures. It is that to which European attention is constantly directed. If a great house becomes bankrupt there, its storehouses are emptied, and the goods are shipped to America, where, in consequence of our auctions, and our custom-house credits, the greatest facilities are afforded in the sale of them. Combinations among manufacturers might take place, or even the operations of foreign governments might be directed to the destruction of our establishments. A repeal, therefore, of one protecting duty, from some one or all of these causes, would be followed by flooding the country with the foreign fabric, surcharging the market, reducing the price, and a complete prostration of our manufactories; after which, the foreigner would leisurely look about to indemnify himself in the increased prices which he would be enabled to command by his monopoly of the supply of our consumption. What American citizen, after the government had displayed this vacillating policy, would be again tempted to place the smallest confidence in the public faith, and adventure, once more, in this branch of industry?

Gentlemen have allowed to the manufacturing portions of the community no peace; they have been constantly threatened with the overthrow of the American System. From the year 1820, if not from 1816, down to this time, they have been held in a condition of constant alarm and insecurity. Nothing is more prejudicial to the great interests of a nation than unsettled and varying policy. Although every appeal to the national legislature has been responded to, in conformity with the wishes and sentiments of the great majority of the people, measures of protection have only been carried by such small majorities, as to excite hopes on the one hand and fears on the other. Let the country breathe; let its vast resources be developed; let its energies be fully put forth; let it have tranquility; and, my word for it, the degree of perfection in the arts which it will exhibit will be greater than that which has been presented, astonishing as our progress has been. Although some branches of our manufactures might, and, in foreign markets, now do, fearlessly contend with similar foreign fabrics, there are many others, yet in their infancy, struggling with the difficulties which encompass them. We should look at the *whole system*, and recollect that time when we contemplate the great movements of a nation, is very different from the short period which is allotted for the duration of individual life. The honorable gentleman from South Carolina well and eloquently said, in 1824, "No great interest of any country ever yet grew up in a day; no new branch of industry can become firmly and profitably established, but in a long course of years; every thing, indeed, great or good, is matured by slow degrees; that which attains a speedy maturity is of small value, and is destined to a brief existence. It is the order of Providence that powers gradually developed shall alone attain permanency and perfection. Thus must it be with our national institutions, and national character itself."

Domestic Market

I feel most sensibly, Mr. President, how much I have trespassed upon the Senate. My apology is, a deep and deliberate conviction that the great cause under debate involves the prosperity and the destiny of the Union. But the best requital I can make for the friendly indulgence which has been extended to me by the Senate, and for which I shall ever retain sentiments of lasting gratitude, is, to proceed with as little delay as practicable, to the conclusion of a discourse which has not been more tedious to the Senate than exhausting to me. I have now to consider the remaining of the two propositions which I have already announced. That is,

2nd. That under the operation of the American System, the products of our agriculture command a higher price than they would do without it, by the creation of a home market; and, by the augmentation of wealth produced by manufacturing industry, which enlarged our powers of consumption, both of domestic and foreign articles. The importance of the home market is among the established maxims which are universally recognized by all writers and all men. However some may differ as to the relative advantages of the foreign and the home market, none deny to the latter great value and high consideration. It is nearer to us, beyond the control of foreign legislation, and undisturbed by those vicissitudes to which all international intercourse is more or less exposed. The most stupid are sensible of the benefit of a residence in the vicinity of a large manufactory, or a market town, of a good road, or of a navigable stream, which connects their farms with some great capital. If the pursuits of all men were perfectly the same, although they would be in possession of the greatest abundance of the particular produce of their industry, they might, at the same time, be in extreme want of other necessary articles of human subsistence. The uniformity of the general occupation would preclude all exchanges—all commerce. It is only in the diversity of the vocations of the members of a community that the means can be found for those salutary exchanges which conduce to the general prosperity; and the greater that diversity, the more extensive and the more animating is the circle of exchange. Even if foreign markets were freely and widely open to the reception of our agricultural produce, from its bulky nature, and the distance of the interior, and the dangers of the ocean, large portions of it could never profitably reach the foreign market. But let us quit this field of theory, clear as it is, and look at the practical operation of the system of protection, beginning with the most valuable staple of our agriculture.

In considering this staple, the first circumstance that excites our surprise is the rapidity with which the amount of it has annually increased. Does not this fact, however, demonstrate that the cultivation of it could not have been so very unprofitable? If the business were ruinous, would more and more have annually engaged in it? The quantity in 1816 was 81 millions of pounds; in 1826, 204 millions; and, in 1830, near 300 millions! The ground of greatest surprise is, that it has been able to sustain even its present price with such an enormous augmentation of quantity. It could not have done it but for the combined operation of three causes, by which the consumption of cotton fabrics has been greatly extended, in consequence of their reduced prices: 1st, competition; 2nd, the improvement of labor-saving machinery; and 3rd, the low price of the raw material. The crop of 1819, amounting to 88 millions of pounds, produced $21 millions; the crop of 1823; when the amount was swelled to 174 millions, (almost double that of 1819) produced a less sum, by more than half a million of dollars; and the crop of 1824, amounting to 30 millions of pounds less than that of the preceding year, produced $1.5 million more.

If there be any foundation for the established law of price, supply, and demand, ought not the fact of this great increase of the supply to account, satisfactorily, for the alleged low price of cotton? Is it necessary to look beyond that *single fa*ct to the tariff—to the diminished produce of the mines furnishing the precious metals, or to any other cause, for the solution? This subject is well understood in the South; and, although I cannot approve the practice which has been introduced, of quoting authority, and still less the authority of newspapers, for favorite theories, I must ask permission of the Senate to read an article from a southern newspaper. [Here Mr. HAYNE requested Mr. CLAY to give the name of the authority, that it might appear whether it was not some other than a *southern pa*per expressing *southern* *se*ntiments. Mr. CLAY stated that it was from the Charleston City Gazette, one, he believed, of the oldest and most respectable prints in that city, although he was not sure what might be its sentiments on the question which at present divides the people of South Carolina.] The article comprises a full explanation of the low price of cotton, and assigns to it its true cause—increased production.

[Mr. C. read the article as follows:]

From the Charleston City Gazette, copied into the New Orleans Emporium, January 4.

1st. The greatest fluctuation in the price of cotton was *before the* tariff of 1824.

2nd. Cotton, like every other article of merchandise, has its fixed price, not in America, but in the market of the world, and depends upon the proportion between demand and supply, just as corn, which, when it is scarce, sells high, and when plenty sells low.

To illustrate how perfectly the price depends on the demand, it is stated that the crop of 1819, amounting to eighty-eight millions of pounds, sold for twenty-one millions of dollars; while the crop of 1823, amounting to one hundred and seventy millions of pounds, was sold for only twenty millions of dollars! And this before the light tariff of 1824. The cause of this difference in the price of cotton is found in the state of the markets, which were hungry in 1819, and had not a great supply, but were overfed in 1823, and could hardly digest the crop of that year.

The price of cotton fluctuated before the present tariff: and, if the same causes of fluctuation exist, they will produce the same effects, independent of the tariff. It is true cotton has come to be sold at ten cents per pound, that used to bring twenty cents. In this reduction of his profits, the cotton planter only shares the same with the wheat grower. Flour is sold at five dollars per barrel, which formerly brought eight and ten dollars; and the products of the earth generally are low, because they are very abundant.

With respect to cotton, this is to be said further. No mode of investing money in agricultural pursuits, this side of the sugar plantations, has afforded so great an income as the culture of cotton. So that has happened to the cotton planter, which happens to all, viz. a diminution of his income, from the multitudes of those who adopted his lucrative business.

To see relief from this depressed price of cotton, by repealing the tariff law, is a most inconsiderate step: for the tariff not only creates a new market for raw cotton, but it also converts some of the finest country for growing cotton into sugar plantations. The tariff, by protecting domestic sugars, enables the Louisianian to raise sugar. Remove the tariff from sugars, and the Louisianian cannot compete with the West Indian. Cotton he can raise to better advantage than the Carolinian. So the relief of the cotton planter, sought by the repeal of the protecting tariff, would multiply cotton growers, and cut off the Northeastern market at one and the same blow. What a stroke of nullifying policy that would be!

The price of any thing in market is governed by the stock in market; if that is great, the price is low; if small, the price is high. Whatever has a tendency to consume the stock, increases the price; and whatever has a tendency to increase the stock, diminishes the price of that article in the market.

The terrible manufactures at the North do not add to the stock of cotton; they diminish the stock, and raise the price in the market of the world. They consume vast quantities of cotton, and clear the market of what might otherwise become a drug. A repeal of the tariff law would wind up the Northern factories. When these cease to be consumers, the price of cotton must fall lower than it now is.

Let us suppose that the home demand for cotton, which has been created by the American System were to cease, and that the 200,000 (14) bales, that the home market now absorbs, were thrown into the glutted markets of foreign countries, would not the effect inevitably be to produce a further and great reduction in the price of the article? If there be any truth in the facts and principles which I have before stated, and endeavored to illustrate, it cannot be doubted that the existence of American manufactures has tended to increase the demand, and extend the consumption of the raw material; and that, but for this increased demand, the price of the article would have fallen, possibly one-half, lower than it now is. The error of the opposite argument is, in assuming one thing, which, being denied, the whole fails; that is, it assumes that the *whole la*bor of the United States would be profitably employed, without manufactures. Now, the truth is, that the system *excites and creates la*bor, and this labor, and this labor creates wealth, and this new wealth communicates additional ability to consume, which acts on all the objects contributing to human comfort and enjoyment. The amount of cotton imported into the two ports of Boston and Providence alone, (during the last year, and it was imported exclusively for the home manufacture) was 109,517 bales.

On passing from that article to others of our agricultural productions, we shall find not less gratifying facts. The total quantity of flour imported into Boston during the same year was 284,504 barrels and 3,955 half barrels; of which there were from Virginia, Georgetown, and Alexandria, 114,222 barrels; of Indian corn, 581,131 bushels; of oats, 239,809 bushels; of rye, about 50,000 bushels; and of shorts, 33,489 bushels. Into the port of Providence, 71,369 barrels of flour, 216,662 bushels of Indian corn, and 7,772 bushels of rye. And there were discharged at the port of Philadelphia 420,353 bushels of Indian corn, 201,878 bushels of wheat, and 110,557 bushels of rye and barley. There were slaughtered in Boston during the same year, 1831 (the only northern city from which I have obtained returns), 33,922 beef cattle, 15,400 stores, 84,453 sheep, and 26,871 swine. It is confidently believed that there is not a less quantity of southern flour consumed at the North than 800,000 barrels—a greater amount, probably, than is shipped to all the foreign markets in the world together.

What would be the condition of the farming country of the United States—of all that portion which lies north, east, and west of James River, including a large part of North Carolina, if a home market did not exist for this immense amount of agricultural produce? Without that market, where could it be sold? In foreign markets? If their restrictive laws did not exist, their *capacity* would not enable them to purchase and consume this vast addition to their present supplies, which must be thrown in, or thrown away, but for the home market. But their laws exclude us from their markets. I shall content myself by calling the attention of the Senate to Great Britain only. The duties, in the ports of the United Kingdom, on bread stuffs, are prohibitory, except in times of dearth. On rice, the duty is fifteen shillings sterling per hundred weight, being more than 100 percent. On manufactured tobacco, it is nine shillings sterling per pound, or about 2,000 percent. On leaf tobacco, three shillings per pound, or 1,200 percent. On lumber and some other articles, they are from 400 to 1,500 percent more than on similar articles imported from the British colonies. In the British West Indies, the duty on beef, pork, hams, and bacon, is twelve shillings sterling per hundred, more than 100 percent on the first cost of beef and pork in the western states. And yet Great

Britain is the power in whose behalf we are called upon to legislate, so that *we may* enable *her to* purchase our cotton! Great Britain, that thinks only of herself in her own legislation! When have we experienced justice, much less favor, at her hands? When did she shape her legislation in reference to the interests of any foreign powers? She is a great, opulent, and powerful nation; but haughty, arrogant, and supercilious. Not more separated from the rest of the world by the sea that girts her island, than she is separated in feeling, sympathy, or friendly consideration of their welfare. Gentlemen, in supposing it impracticable that we should successfully compete with her in manufactures, do injustice to the skill and enterprise of their own country. Gallant as Great Britain undoubtedly is, we have gloriously contended with her, man to man, gun to gun, ship to ship, fleet to fleet, and army to army. And I have no doubt we are destined to achieve equal success in the more useful, if not nobler contest, for superiority in the arts of civil life.

I could extend and dwell on the long list of articles— the hemp, iron, lead, coal, and other items, for which a demand is created in the home market, by the operation of the American System; but I should exhaust the patience of the Senate. *Where, where,* should we find a market for all these articles, if it did not exist at home? What would be the condition of the largest portion of our people and of the territory, if this home market were annihilated? How could they be supplied with objects of prime necessity? What would not be the certain and inevitable decline in the price of all these articles, but for the home market? And allow me, Mr. President, to say, that, of all the agricultural parts of the United States which are benefited by the operation of this system, none are equally so with those which border the Chesapeake Bay, the lower parts of North Carolina, Virginia, and the two shores of Maryland. Their facilities of transportation and proximity to the North give them decided advantages.

But if all this reasoning were totally fallacious—if the price of manufactured articles were really higher under the American System, than without it, I should still argue that high or low prices were themselves relative—relative to the ability to pay them. It is in vain to tempt, to tantalize us with the lower prices of European fabrics than our own, if we have nothing wherewith to purchase them. If, by the home exchanges, we can be supplied with necessary, even if they are dearer and worse, articles of American production than the foreign, it is better than not to be supplied at all. And how would the large portion of our country which I have described, be supplied, but for the home exchanges? A poor people destitute of wealth or of exchangeable commodities, has nothing to purchase foreign fabrics. To them they are equally beyond their reach, whether their cost be a dollar or a guinea. It is in this view of the matter that Great Britain, by her vast wealth—her *exerted and protected* industry—is enabled to bear a burden of taxation which, when compared to that of other nations, appears enormous; but which, when her immense riches are compared to theirs, is light and trivial. The gentleman from South Carolina has drawn a lively and flattering picture of our coasts, bays, rivers, and harbors; and he argues that these proclaimed the design of Providence that we should be a commercial people. I agree with him. We differ only as to the means. He would cherish the foreign, and neglect the internal trade. I would foster both. What is navigation without ships, or ships without cargoes? By penetrating the bosoms of our mountains, and extracting from them their precious treasures; by cultivating the earth, and *securing a* home market for its rich and abundant products; by employing the water power with which we are blessed; by stimulating and protecting our native industry, in all its forms; we shall but nourish and promote the prosperity of commerce, foreign and domestic.

I have hitherto considered the question in reference only to a state of peace; but a season of war ought not to be entirely overlooked. We have enjoyed near twenty years of peace; but who can tell when the storm of war shall again break forth? Have we forgotten, so soon, the privations to which not merely our brave soldiers and our gallant tars were subjected, but the whole community, during the last war, for the want of absolute necessaries? To what an enormous price they rose? And how inadequate the supply was, at any price? The statesman, who justly elevates his views, will look behind as well as forward, and at the existing state of things; and he will graduate the policy which he recommends, to all the probable exigencies which may arise in the republic. Taking this comprehensive range, it would be easy to show that the higher prices of peace, if prices were higher in peace, were more than compensated by the lower prices of war, during which supplies of all essential articles are indispensable to its vigorous, effectual, and glorious prosecution. I conclude this part of the argument with the hope that my humble exertions have not been altogether unsuccessful in showing—

1. That the policy which we have been considering out to continue to be regarded as the genuine American System.

2. That the free trade system, which is proposed as its substitute, ought really to be considered the British colonial system.

3. That the American System is beneficial to all parts of the Union, and absolutely necessary to much the

larger portion.

4. That the price of the great staple of cotton, and of all our chief productions of agriculture, has been sustained and upheld, and a decline averted by the protective system.

5. That, if the foreign demand for cotton has been at all diminished by the operation of that system, the diminution has been more than compensated in the additional demand created at home.

6. That the constant tendency of the system, by creating competition among ourselves, and between American and European industry, reciprocally acting upon each other, is to reduce prices of manufactured objects.

7. That, in point of fact, objects within the scope of the policy of protection have greatly fallen in price.

8. That if, in a season of peace, these benefits are experienced in a season of war, when the foreign supply might be cut off, they would be much more extensively felt.

9. And, finally, that the substitution of the British colonial system for the American System, without benefiting any section of the Union, by subjecting us to a foreign legislation, regulated by foreign interests, would lead to the prostration of our manufactures, general impoverishment, and ultimate ruin.

Rule by Majority

And now, Mr. President, I have to make a few observations on a delicate subject, which I approach with all the respect that is due to its serious and grave nature. They have not, indeed, been rendered necessary by the speech of the gentleman from South Carolina, whose forbearance to notice the topic was commendable, as his argument throughout was characterized by an ability and dignity worthy of him and of the Senate. The gentleman made one declaration, which might possibly be misinterpreted, and I submit to him whether an explanation of it be not proper. The declaration, as reported in his printed speech, is, "the instinct of self interest might have taught us an easier way of relieving ourselves from this oppression. It wanted but the will to have supplied ourselves with every article embraced in the protective system, free of duty, without any other participation, on our part than a simple consent to receive them." [Here Mr. HAYNE rose, and remarked that the passages, which immediately preceded and followed the paragraph cited, he thought, plainly indicated his meaning, which related to evasions of the system, by illicit introduction of goods, which they were not disposed to countenance in South

Carolina.] I am happy to hear this explanation. But, sir, it is impossible to conceal from our view the facts that there is great excitement in South Carolina; that the protective system is openly and violently denounced in popular meetings; and that the legislature itself has declared its purpose of resorting to counteracting measures—a suspension of which has only been submitted to, for the purpose of allowing Congress time to *retrace its* steps. With respect to this Union, Mr. President, the truth cannot be too generally proclaimed, nor too strongly inculcated, that it is necessary to the *whole and* to all the *parts*—necessary to those parts, indeed, in different degrees, but vitally necessary to *each;* and that threats to disturb or dissolve it, coming from any of the parts, would be quite as indiscreet and improper, as would be threats from the residue to exclude those parts from the pale of its benefits. The great principle, which lies at the foundation of all free government, is, that the majority must govern; from which there is or can be no appeal but to the sword. That majority ought to govern wisely, equitably, moderately, and constitutionally, but govern *it must,* subject only to that terrible appeal. If ever one, or several states, being a minority, can, by menacing a dissolution of the Union, succeed in forming an abandonment of great measures deemed essential to the interests and prosperity of the whole, the Union, from that moment, is practically gone. It may linger on, in form and name, but its vital spirit has fled forever! Entertaining these deliberate opinions, I would entreat the patriotic people of South Carolina—the land of Marion, Sumpter, and Pickens—of Rutledge, Laurens, the Pinckneys, and Lowndes—of living and present names, which I would mention if they were not living or present—to pause, solemnly pause! And contemplate the frightful precipice which lies directly before them. To retreat may be painful and mortifying to their gallantry and pride, but it is to retreat to the Union, to safety, and to those brethren, with whom, or with whose ancestors, they, or their ancestors, have won, on fields of glory, imperishable renown. To advance, is to rush on certain and inevitable disgrace and destruction.

We have been told of deserted castles, of uninhabited halls, and of mansions, once the seats of opulence and hospitality, now abandoned and mouldering in ruins. I never had the honor of being in South Carolina; but I have heard and read of the stories of its chivalry, and of its generous and openhearted liberality. I have heard, too, of the struggle for power between the lower and upper country. The same causes which existed in Virginia, with which I have been acquainted, I presume, have had their influence in Carolina. In whose hands now are the once proud seats of Westover, Curles, Maycocks, Shirley, (15) and others, on James River, and in lower Virginia? Under the operation of laws abolishing the principle of primogeniture, and providing the equitable rule of an equal distribution of estates among those in equal degree of consanguinity, they have passed into other and stranger hands. Some of the descendants of illustrious families have gone to the far West, whilst others, lingering behind, have contrasted their present condition with that of their venerated ancestors. They behold themselves excluded from their fathers' houses, now in the hands of those who were once their fathers' overseers, or sinking into decay; their imaginations paint ancient renown, the fading honors of their name, glories gone by; too poor to live, too proud to work, too high-minded and honorable to resort to ignoble means of acquisition, brave, daring, chivalrous, *what can* be the cause of their present unhappy state? The "accursed tariff" presents itself to their excited imaginations, and they blindly rush into the ranks of those who, unfurling the banner of nullification, would place a state upon its sovereignty! The danger to our Union does not lie on the side of persistence in the American System, but on that of its abandonment. If, as I have supposed and believe, the inhabitants of all north and east of James River, and all west of the mountains, including Louisiana, are deeply interested in the preservation of that system, would they be reconciled to its overthrow? Can it be expected that two-thirds, if not three-fourths, of the people of the United States would consent to the destruction of a policy believed to be indispensably necessary to their prosperity? When, too, this sacrifice is made at the instance of a single interest, which they verily believe will not be promoted by it? In estimating the degree of peril which may be incident to two opposite courses of human policy, the statesman would be short-sighted who should content himself with viewing only the evils, real or imaginary, which belong to that course which is in practical operation. He should lift himself up to the contemplation of those greater and more certain dangers which might inevitably attend the adoption of the alternative course. What would be the condition of this Union, if Pennsylvania and New York, those mammoth members of our confederacy, were firmly persuaded that their industry was paralyzed, and their prosperity blighted, by the enforcement of the British colonial system, under the delusive name of free trade? They are now tranquil, and happy, and contented, conscious of their welfare, and feeling a salutary and rapid circulation of the products of home manufactures and home industry throughout all their great arteries. But let that be checked, let them feel that a foreign system is to predominate, and the sources of their subsistence and comfort dried up; let New England and the West, and the middle states, all feel that they too are the victims of a mistaken policy, and let these vast portions of our country despair of any favorable change, and then, indeed, might we tremble for the continuance and safety of this Union!

And need I remind you, sir, that this dereliction of the duty of protecting our domestic industry, and abandonment of it to the fate of foreign legislation, would be directly at war with leading considerations which prompted the adoption of the present constitution? The states, respectively, surrendered to the general government the whole power of laying imposts on foreign goods. They stripped themselves of all power to protect their own manufactures, by the most efficacious means of encouragement—the imposition of duties on rival foreign fabrics. Did they create that great trust? Did they voluntarily subject themselves to this self-restriction, that the power should remain in the federal government, inactive, unexecuted, and lifeless? Mr. Madison, (16) at the commencement of the government, told you otherwise. In discussing, at that early period, this very subject, he declared that a failure to exercise this power would be a *"fraud"* upon the northern states, to which may now be added the middle and western states.

[Mr. MILLER (17) asked to what expression of Mr. Madison's opinion Mr. CLAY referred; and Mr. C.

replied, his opinion, expressed in the House of Representatives, in 1789, as reported in Lloyd's Congressional Debates.]

Gentlemen are greatly deceived as to the hold which this system has in the affections of the people of the United States. They resent that it is the policy of New England, and that she is most benefited by it. If there be any part of this Union which has been most steady, most unanimous, and most determined in its support, it is Pennsylvania. Why is not that powerful state attacked? Why pass her over, and aim the blow at New England? New England came, reluctantly, into the policy. In 1824, a majority of her delegation was opposed to it. From the largest state of New England there was but a solitary vote in favor of the bill. That enterprising people can readily accommodate their industry to any policy, provided it be *settled*. They supposed this was fixed, and they submitted to the decrees of government. And the progress of public opinion has kept pace with the development of the benefits of the system. Now, all New England, at least in this house, (with the exception of *one small, still voice)* [Mr. HILL, (18) of New Hampshire] is in favor of the System. In 1824, all Maryland was against it; now, the majority is for it. Then, Louisiana, with one exception, was opposed to it; now, without any exception, she is in favor of it. The march of public sentiment is to the South. Virginia will be the next convert; and, in less than seven years, if there be no obstacles from political causes, or prejudices industriously instilled, the majority of eastern Virginia will be, as the majority of western Virginia now is, in favor of the American System. North Carolina will follow later, but not less certainly. Eastern Tennessee is now in favor of the system. And, finally, its doctrines will pervade the whole Union, and the wonder will be that they ever should have been opposed.

Objections Addressed

I have now to proceed to notice some objections which have been urged against the resolution under consideration. With respect to the amendment which the gentleman from South Carolina had offered, as he has intimated his purpose to modify it, I shall forbear, for the present, to comment upon it. It is contended that the resolution proposes the repeal of duties on luxuries, leaving those on necessaries to remain, and that it will, therefore, relieve the rich, without lessening the burdens of the poor. And the gentleman from South Carolina has carefully selected, for ludicrous effect, a number of the unprotected articles;

cosmetics, perfumes, oranges, etc. I must say that his exhibition of the gentleman is not in keeping with the candor which he has generally displayed; that he knows very well that the duties upon these articles are trifling, and that it is of little consequence whether they are repealed or retained. Both systems, the American and the foreign, comprehend some articles which may be deemed luxuries. The Senate knows that the unprotected articles which yield the principal part of the revenue, with which this measure would dispense, are coffee, tea, spices, wines, and silks. Of all these articles, wines and silks alone can be pronounced luxuries; and as to wines, we have already ratified a treaty, not yet promulgated, by which the duties on them are to be considerably reduced. If the universality of the use of objects of consumption determines their classification, coffee, tea, and spices, in the present condition of civilized society, may be considered necessaries. Even if they were luxuries, why should not the poor, by cheapening their prices, if that can be effected, be allowed to use them? Why should not a poor man be allowed to tie a silk handkerchief on his neck, occasionally regale himself with a glass of cheap French wine, or present his wife or daughter with a silk gown, to be worn on Sabbath or gala days? I am quite sure that I do not misconstrue the feelings of the gentleman's heart, in supposing that he would be happy to see the poor, as well as the rich, moderately indulging themselves in these innocent gratifications. For one, I am delighted to see the condition of the poor attracting the consideration of the opponents of the tariff. It is for the great body of the people, and especially for the poor, that I have ever supported the American System. It affords them profitable employment, and supplies the means of comfortable subsistence. It *secures to* them, certainly, necessaries of life manufactured at home, and places within their reach, and enables them to acquire, a reasonable share of foreign luxuries; whilst the system of gentlemen *promises the*m necessaries made in foreign countries, and which are beyond their power, and *denies to* them luxuries which they would possess no means to purchase.

The constant complaint of South Carolina against the tariff, is, that it checks importations, and disables foreign powers from purchasing the agricultural productions of the United States. The effect of the resolution will be to increase importations, not so much, it is true from Great Britain, as from other powers, but not the less acceptable on that account. It is a misfortune that so large a portion of our foreign commerce concentrates in one nation; it subjects us too much to the legislation and the policy of that nation, and exposes us to the influence of her numerous agents, factors, and merchants. And it is not among the smallest recommendations of the measure before the Senate, that its tendency will be to expand our commerce with France—our great revolutionary ally—the land of our Lafayette. There is much greater probability, also of an enlargement of the present demand for cotton, in France, than in Great Britain. France engaged later in the manufacture of cotton, and has made, therefore, less progress. She has, moreover, no colonies producing the article in abundance, whose industry she might be tempted to encourage.

The honorable gentleman from Maryland, [Mr. SMITH] by his reply to a speech, which on the opening of the subject of this resolution, I had occasion to make, has rendered it necessary that I should take some notice of his observations. The honorable gentleman stated that he had been *accused of* partiality to the manufacturing interest. Never was there a more groundless and malicious charge preferred against a calumniated man. Since this question has been agitated in the public councils, although I have often heard from him professions of attachment to this branch of industry, I have never known any member a more uniform, determined, and uncompromising opponent of them, than the honorable senator has invariably been. And if, hereafter, the calumny should be repeated, of his friendship to the American System, I shall be ready to furnish to him, in the most solemn manner, my testimony to his innocence. The honorable gentleman supposed that I had advanced the idea that the *permanent revenue* of this country should be fixed at $18 millions. Certainly I had no intention to announce such an opinion, nor do my explanations, fairly interpreted, imply it. I stated, on the occasion referred to, that estimating the ordinary revenue of the country at $25 millions, and the amount of the duties on the unprotected articles proposed to be repealed by the resolution, at $7 millions, the latter sum taken from the former would leave $18. But I did not intimate any belief that the revenue of the country ought, for the future, to be permanently fixed at that or any other precise sum. I stated that, after having effected so great a reduction, we might pause, cautiously survey the whole ground, and deliberately determine upon other measures of reduction, some of which I indicated. And I now say, preserve the protective system in full vigor, give us the proceeds of the public domain for internal improvements, or, if you please, partly for that object, and partly for the removal of the free blacks, with their own consent, from the United States; and, for one, I have no objection to the reduction of the public revenue to $15, to $13, or even to $9 millions.

In regard to the scheme of the secretary of the treasury for paying off the whole of the remaining public debt by the 4th of March, 1833, including the 3 percent, and, for that purpose, selling the bank stock, I had remarked that, with the exception of the 3 percent, there was not more than about $4 millions of the debt due and payable within this year; that, to meet this, the secretary had stated, in his annual report, that the treasury would have, from the receipts of this year, $14 millions, applicable to the principal of the debt; that I did not perceive any urgency for paying off the 3 percent by the precise day suggested; and that there was no necessity, according to the plans of the treasury, assuming them to be expedient and proper, to postpone the repeal of the duties on unprotected articles. The gentleman from Maryland imputed to me *ignorance of* the act of the 24th April 1830, according to which, in his opinion, the secretary was *obliged to* purchase the 3 percent. On what ground the senator supposed I was *ignorant of* that act, he has not stated. Although, when it passed, I was at Ashland, I assure him that I was not there altogether uninformed of what was passing in the world. I regularly received the *Register* (19) of my excellent friend Mr. Niles, published in Baltimore, the *National Intelligencer,* and other papers. There are two errors to which gentlemen are sometimes liable: one is to magnify the amount of knowledge which they possess themselves, and the second is to depreciate that which others have acquired. And will the gentleman from Maryland excuse me for thinking that no man is more prone to commit both errors than himself? I will I will not say that he is *ignorant of* the true meaning of the act of 1830, but I certainly place a different construction upon it from what he does. It does not *oblige the* secretary of the treasury, or rather the commissioners of the Sinking Fund, to apply the surplus of any year to the purchase of the 3-percent stock particularly, but leaves them at liberty "to apply such surplus to the purchase of *any po*rtion of the public debt, at such rates as, in their opinion, may be advantageous to the United States." This vests a *discretionary au*thority, to be exercised under official responsibility. And if any secretary of the treasury, when he had the option of purchasing a portion of the debt, bearing a higher rate of interest, at par or about par, were to execute the act by purchasing the 3 percent at its present price, he would merit impeachment. Undoubtedly a state of facts may exist, such as there being no public debt remaining to be paid but the 3-percent stock, with a surplus in the treasury, idle and unproductive, in which it might be expedient to apply that surplus to the reimbursement of the 3 percents. But, whilst the interest of money is at a greater rate than 3 percent, it would not, I think, be wise to produce an accumulation of public treasure for such a purpose. The postponement of any reduction of the amount of the revenue, at this session, must however give rise to that very accumulation; and it is, therefore, that I cannot perceive the utility of the postponement.

We are told by the gentleman from Maryland, that offers have been made to the secretary of the treasury to exchange 3 percents at their market price of 96 percent for the bank stock of the government at its market price, which is about 126 and he thinks it would be wise to accept them. If the charter of the bank is renewed, that stock will be probably worth much more than its present price; if not renewed, much less. Would it be fair in government, whilst the question is pending and undecided, to make such an exchange? The difference in value between a stock bearing 3 percent and one bearing 7 percent, must be really much greater than the difference between 96 and 1126 percent. Supposing them to be perpetual annuities, the one would be worth more than twice the value of the other. But my objection to the treasury plan is, that it is not necessary to execute it— to continue these duties, as the secretary proposes. The secretary has a debt of $24 millions to pay; he has, from the accruing *receipts of* this year, $14 millions; and we are now told by the senator from Maryland that this sum of $14 millions is exclusive of any of the *duties ac*cruing this year. He proposes to raise $8 millions by a sale lf the bank stock, and to anticipate, from the revenues receivable next year, $2 millions more. These three items then, of $14 millions, $8 millions, and $2 millions, make up the sum required of $24 millions, without the aid of the duties to which the resolution relates.

The gentleman from Maryland insists that the general government has been liberal towards the West in its appropriations of public lands for internal improvements; and, as to fortifications, he contends that the expenditures near the mouth of the Mississippi are for its especial benefit. The appropriations of land to the states of Ohio, Indiana, Illinois, and Alabama, have been liberal; but it is not to be overlooked that the general government is itself the greatest proprietor of land, and that a tendency of the improvements, which these appropriations were to effect, is to increase the value of the unsold public domain. The erection of the fortifications for the defence of Louisiana was highly proper; but the gentleman might as well place to the account of the West the disbursements for the fortifications intended to defend Baltimore, Philadelphia, and New York, to all which capitals western produce is sent, and in security of all of which the western people feel a lively interest. They do not object to expenditures for the army, for the navy, for fortifications, or for any other defensive or commercial object on the Atlantic, but they do think that their condition ought also to receive friendly attention from the general government. With respect to the state of Kentucky, not one cent of money, or one acre of land, has been applied to any object of internal improvement within her limits. The subscription to the stock of the canal at Louisville was for an object in which many states were interested. The senator from Maryland complains that he has been unable to obtain any aid for the railroad which the enterprise of Baltimore has projected, and, in part, executed. That was a great work, the conception of which was bold and highly honorable, and it deserves national encouragement. But how has the Committee of Roads and Canals, at this session, been constituted? The senator from Maryland possessed a brief authority to organize it, and, if I am not misinformed, a majority of the members composing it, appointed by him, are opposed both to the constitutionality of the power and the expediency of exercising it.

To the Friends of the American System

And now, sir, I would address a few words to the friends of the American System in the Senate. The revenue *must, ought to* be reduced. The country will not, after, by the payment of the public debt, $10 or

$12 millions become unnecessary, bear such an annual surplus. Its distribution would form a subject of perpetual contention. Some of the opponents of the system understand the stratagem by which to attack it, and are shaping their course accordingly. It is to crush the system by the accumulation of revenue, and by the effort to persuade the people that they are unnecessarily *taxed*, whilst those would really *tax them* who would break up the *native* sources of supply, and render them dependent upon the *foreign*. But the revenue *ought to* be reduced, so as to accommodate it to the fact of the payment of the public debt. And the alternative is, or may be, to *preserve the* protecting system, and repeal the duties on the *unprotected* articles, or to preserve the duties on *unprotected* articles, and endanger, if not *destroy*, the system. Let us then adopt the measure before us, which will benefit all classes: the farmer, the professional man, the merchant, the manufacturer, the mechanic, and the cotton planter more than all. A few months ago, there was no diversity of opinion as to the expediency of this measure. All, then, seemed to unite in the selection of these objects, for a repeal of duties which were not produced within the country. Such a repeal did not touch our domestic industry, violated no principle, offended no prejudice.

Can we not all, whatever may be our favorite theories, cordially unite on this *neutral* ground? When

that is occupied, let us look beyond it, and see if anything can be done, in the field of protection, to modify, to improve it, or to satisfy those who are opposed to the system. Our southern brethren believe that it is injurious to them, and ask its repeal. We believe that its abandonment will be prejudicial to them, and *ruinous to* every other section of the Union. However strong their convictions may be, they are not stronger than ours. Between the points of the preservation of the system and its absolute repeal, there is no principle of union. If it can be *shown to* operate immoderately on any quarter; if the measure of protection to any article can be demonstrated to be undue and inordinate, it would be the duty of Congress to interpose and apply a remedy. And none will cooperate more heartily than I shall, in the performance of that duty. It is quite probable that beneficial modifications of the system may be made, without impairing it efficacy. But, to make it fulfill the purposes of its institution, the measure of protection ought to be adequate. If it be not, all interests will be injuriously affected. The manufacturer, crippled in his exertions, will produce less perfect and dearer fabrics, and the consumer will feel the consequence. This is the spirit, and these are the principles only, on which it seems to me that a settlement of this great question can be made satisfactorily to all parts of our Union.
[The delivery of the above speech of Mr. CLAY

occupied portions of three several days; but the whole is embodied here, unbroken.]

<u>Free Trade Religion</u>

(To the tune of Old Time Religion)

Give me that Free Trade religion
Give me that Free Trade religion
Give me that old Free Trade religion
Cause they says it's good for me

Adam Smith is the father of Free Trade
Wrote a book about the wealth of nations
Had some funny idea about payin' folks
But it must be good for me

Oh a slave is worth twice his maintenance
He worth double what it cost to keep him
They're a bargain so you better get some
Boss man reckons he'll buy three

Oh a free man will cost you double
Cause O' his wife and their four childrens
Because two of them will die
Before they reach maturity

(Chorus)

Oh Republicans love the Free Trade
And the Democrats love the Free Trade

And the Tea Party love the Free Trade
Oh it makes them giggly

Oh the Boehner love the Free Trade
And Obama love the Free Trade
Yeah Pelosi love the Free Trade
More than Xanax well nearly

Oh the Walmart love the Free Trade
Cause they give out them low prices
Saved America so much money
That we're broke now don't you see

(Chorus)

Kim Jung il love the Free Trade
Gives his folks ten year vacations
They timber in Siberia
To sell Great Britain trees

Alexander Hamilton didn't like Free Trade
Abraham Lincoln fought again' Free Trade
President McKinley hated Free Trade
They all died for liberty

President Kennedy didn't mind Free Trade
But he printed some debt free money
And that's worse than hatin' Free Trade

So they killed him on teevee

(Chorus)

The Federal Reserve love the Free Trade
Said Smoot-Hawley was a villain
Ben Bernanke said it was the Fed
But gave apology

Wall Street love the Free Trade
And economists love the Free Trade
We have outsourced all our products
So we have no factories

Celebrities love the Free Trade
With their name on fancy garments
The orphans burned up at the plant
Oops we are so sorry

Take your Free Trade Religion
And go pound salt up yer
Ask me what we really need
Domestic industry

***

ABOUT THE AUTHOR

I was born in Columbus, Ohio to parents of Irish and Scottish descent who grew up in Southern West Virginia. Although not from West Virginia, I got here as quick as I could and grew up in the southern part of the state from 1964 to present where I live with my wife Kimberly, our several pets, and a 1947 Ford tractor. For thirty-nine years I've worked at a variety of vocations including the oilfield and flight simulation software design. I had ten award winning commercial software titles within a four year period as add-ons for Microsoft Flight Simulator, including the Spirit of St. Louis which was used by the Experimental Aircraft Association in Oshkosh, Wisconsin to commemorate the 75th anniversary and reenactment of Charles Lindbergh's historic transatlantic flight. Battered Nation Syndrome was my first book.

In Defense of The American System

Free Trade Religion

Notes

Introduction
The primary source material for the Introduction are from the Library of Congress, and Classic Senate Speeches from the United States Senate.
1. The Atlantic Magazine, Charles Fishman, The Insourcing Boom, December 2012 Issue
2. Henry Clay, *The Senate, 1789-1989: Classic Speeches, In Defense of the American System 1830-1993.*

Chapter One: The Greatest Alexander
Information in this chapter is derived from The Federalist Papers, Alexander Hamilton, by Charles A. Conant, Alexander Hamilton's, Report on Manufactures, and Adam Smith's book, The Wealth of Nations.
1. Soderbaum, Dr. Peter, *Post-Autistic Economics Review*, Sept 2007
2. Smith, Adam, *Wealth of Nations*, 1776
3. Ibid
4. Ibid
5. Ibid
6. Ibid
7. Ibid
8. Ibid
9. Ibid
10. Ibid

11. Ibid

12. Conant, Charles A. Alexander Hamilton, 1901

11. Ibid

12. Ibid

13. Ibid

14. Ibid

15. Ibid

16. Ibid

17. Ibid

18. Williamson, Samuel H. "Seven Ways to Compute the Relative Value of a U.S. Dollar Amount, 1774 to present," MeasuringWorth, April 2013. http://www.measuringworth.com/uscompare/index.php>.

19. Alexander Hamilton, "Report on Manufactures", December 5, 1791

20. Ibid

Chapter Two: The Law of Comparative Advantage
Information in this chapter is derived from the Library of Congress, and Classic Senate Speeches from the United States Senate.

1. William McKinley speech, October 4, 1892 in Boston, MA William McKinley Papers (Library of Congress)

2. Henry Clay, *The Senate, 1789-1989: Classic Speeches, In Defense of the American System 1830-1993*. Washington, D.C.: Government Printing Office, 1994.

3. Ibid

Chapter Three: Free Trade Slavery
Most of the source materials for this chapter were from a documentary made by Vice Media on North Korean Labor Camps, CBS News, the International Labor Organization's attempts to combat forced labor, and a report by The Daily Beast on forced labor slaves in the Malaysian computer industry.
1. Vice Media Inc. www.vice.com, *North Korean Labor Camps*
2. Bangladesh Factory Fire, CBS News
3. Wealth of Nations, Adam Smith, 1776
4. Ibid
5. The Daily Beast, *Bottom of the Barrel: Millions of Asian workers producing goods sold here are trapped in servitude*. Erika Kinetz, March 15, 2008
6. International Labor Organization, www.ilo.org, *Special Action Programme to Combat Forced Labor*
7. Dial, Roger L. *Battered Nation Syndrome*, 2012
8. Washington Monthly, *The Myth of American Productivity*, Michael Mandel, January/February 2012 Issue

Chapter Four: Free Trade Morality
The majority of the information used for this chapter is from Henry Clay's speech on the Senate floor in February, 1832, In Defense of the American System,

the Tariff History of the United States by F.W. Taussig, and The American Pageant, by Thomas A. Bailey.

1. http://www.hillmanfoundation.org/blog/corporations-seeking-job-creation-tax-breaks-hide-outsourcing-stats-with-government-help

2. Taussig, F.W., *The Tariff History of the United States, Part I, Fifth Edition*, G. P. Putnam's Sons, 1910

3. Bailey, Thomas A. *The American Pageant* D.C. Heath and Co. (1971)

Chapter Five: Impetus of War
Most of the source materials for this chapter came from Henry Clay's speech defending the American System, and from contributing authors to A Nation Divided, William W. Freehling, Eric Foner, and edited by George M. Fredrickson.

1. Fredrickson, George M., Freehling, William W., Foner, Eric, *A Nation Divided, Burgess Publishing* Company (1975)

Chapter Six: Common Sense
The majority of source material for this chapter is from my book, Battered Nation Syndrome, including the Chrysler announcement of manufacturing automobiles in China, and the Edmunds expose on the Cash for Clunkers program.

1. Dial, Roger L. *Battered Nation Syndrome,* 2012
2. blog.chryslerllc.com
3. www.edmunds.com, *Cash for Clunkers*
4. Top Gear, Series 18, Episode 2, BBC
5. 2012 Statistic Brain Research Institute. "Job Outsourcing Statistics-Statistic Brain". July 2012. Statistic Brain. March 2013. http://www.statisticbrain.com/outsourcing-statistics-by-country/>.

Chapter Seven: The Way We Were
The material for this chapter is from the Preamble to the U.S. Constitution, current and historical gold and silver prices, and U.S. tariff history from the U.S. Census Bureau.
1. United States Constitution, *Preamble* to the U.S. Constitution

Chapter Eight: A Rising Tide Raises All Ships
1. Bangladesh vs. the U.S.: How much does it cost to make a denim shirt? CNN Staff, May 3, 2013

Chapter Nine: Versus
The material for this chapter comes from arguments in favor of free trade made by various economists, and from speeches made by President William McKinley.
1. William McKinley speech, October 4, 1892 in

Boston, *MA William McKinley Papers* (Library of Congress)

Chapter Ten: Henry Clay
The primary source materials for this chapter come from Classic Senate Speeches from the United States Senate.
1. Robert C. Byrd, *The Senate, 1789-1989: Classic Speeches, 1830-1993*. Washington, D.C.: Government Printing Office, 1994.

Chapter Eleven: Henry Clay's Speech
This chapter contains Henry Clay's three-day speech in February, 1832, in its entirety.
1. U.S. Congress, Senate, Register of Debates in Congress, 22nd Congress, 1st Session, pp. 257-295.
2. Robert Y. Hayne (1791-1839) served in the Senate, 1823-1832.
3. To say nothing of the cotton produced in other foreign countries, the cultivation of this article, of a very superior quality, is constantly extending in the adjacent Mexican province; and, but for the duty, probably a large amount would be introduced into the United States, down Red River and along the coast of the Gulf of Mexico [Clay note]
4. Alexander J. Dallas (1759-1817) was Secretary of the Treasury, 1814-1816.
5. Henry Baldwin of Pennsylvania (1780-1844) served

in the House of Representatives, 1817-1822. In 1830 he was appointed to the Supreme Court by Andrew Jackson.

6. John C. Calhoun of South Carolina (1752-1850), Vice President of the U.S. from 1825-1832, was presiding over the Senate at the time.

7. Mr. Clay has been since reminded that the objection, in the same way, was first urged in the debate of 1820. [Clay note]

8. Eldred Simkins of South Carolina (1779-1831) served in the House of Representatives, 1818-1821.

9. Albert Gallatin of Pennsylvania (1761-1849) served in the Senate, 1793-1794. In 1832 he drafted the message to Congress from the free trade convention in Philadelphia.

10. Mr. Clay subsequently understood that Colonel Murray was a merchant [Clay note]

11. Frederick John Robinson, Viscount Goderich (1782-1859), Prime Minister of England, 1827-1828.

12. Samuel Smith (1752-1839) served in the Senate, 1803-1815 and 1822-1833.

13. Nathaniel Silsbee (1773-1850) served in the Senate, 1826-1835.

14. Mr. Clay stated that he assumed the quantity which was generally computed, but he believed it much greater, and subsequent information justifies his belief. It appears, from the report of the Cotton Committee, appointed by the New York Convention,

that partial returns show a consumption of upwards of 250,000 bales; that the cotton manufacture employs near 40,000 females, and about 5,000 children; that the total dependents on it are 131,489; that the annual wages paid are $12,155,723; the annual value of its products, $32,036,760; the capital, $44,914,984; the number of mills, 795; of spindles, 1,246,503; and of cloth made, 2260,461,990 yards. This statement does not comprehend the western manufactures. [Clay note]

15. As to Shirley, Mr. Clay acknowledges his mistake, made in the warmth of debate. It is yet the abode of the respectable and hospitable descendants of its former opulent proprietor. [Clay note]

16. James Madison (1751-1836), delegate from Virginia to the Constitutional Convention in 1787, served in the House of Representatives, 1789-1797, and as president of the United States, 1809-1817.

17. Stephen D. Miller of South Carolina (1787-1838) served in the Senate, 1831-1833.

18. Isaac Hill (1789-1851) served in the Senate, 1831-1836.

19. Niles' Weekly Register.

Bibliographical Notes

Research for this book was drawn from a variety of sources, including documents from archives, books, news, and magazine articles. It's important to give credit to the writers from whose work I've borrowed. Any errors are mine and mine alone.

2012 Statistic Brain Research Institute. "Job Outsourcing Statistics-Statistic Brain". July 2012. Statistic Brain. March 2013. http://www.statisticbrain.com/outsourcing-statistics-by-country/>.

BLS. "INTERNATIONAL COMPARISONS OF HOURLY COMPENSATION COSTS IN MANUFACTURING, 2011". BLS. December 2012. Bureau of Labor Statistics. March 2013. http://www.bls.gov/news.release/pdf/ichcc.pdf>.

Bureau of Labor Statistics. "Labor Force Statistics from the Current Population Survey". United States Department of Labor. March 2013. http://data.bls.gov/timeseries/LNS14000000>.

Byrd, Robert C. "The American System". United States Senate. 1993. U.S. Government Printing Office. March 2013. http://www.senate.gov/artandhistory/history/resourc es/pdf/AmericanSystem.pdf>.

Edmunds. "Cash for Clunkers Results Finally In". Edmunds. October 2009. Edmunds. March 2013. http://www.edmunds.com/about/press/cash-for-clunkers-results-finally-in-taxpayers-paid-24000-per-vehicle-sold-reports-edmundscom.html>.

Fishman, Charles. "The Insourcing Boom". The

Atlantic. December 2012. The Atlantic. March 2013. http://www.theatlantic.com/magazine/archive/2012/1 2/the-insourcing-boom/309166/>.

Government Accountability Office. "Unemployed Older Workers". GAO. April, 2012. GAO. March 2013. http://www.gao.gov/assets/600/590408.pdf>.

Hamilton, Alexander. First Report on the Public Credit: Treasury Department, January 1790

Hamilton, Alexander; Jay, John; Madison, James. Los Angeles: Sweetwater Press, 2010

Hamilton, Alexander. Report on the Subject of Manufactures: Treasury Department, December 1791

Kinetz, Erika; Wehrfritz, George; Kent, Jonathan. "Bottom of the Barrel". The Daily Beast. March 2008. Newsweek Magazine. March 2013. http://www.thedailybeast.com/newsweek/2008/03/15/ bottom-of-the-barrel.html>.

Malone, Sean W. "The Rise and Fall of the U.S. Dollar". Zero Hedge. August 2009. Mises Institute. March 2013. http://www.zerohedge.com/article/rise-and-fall-us-dollar>.

McMillan, Jack. "Tariffs Not Slavery". Dixie Outfitters. 2002. Dixie Outfitters. March 2013. http://dixieoutfitters.com/p/tariffs-not-slavery>.

Rothbard, Murray N. "Protectionism and the Destruction of Prosperity". Ludwig von Mises Institute. 1986. Ludwig von Mises Institute. http://mises.org/rothbard/protectionism.asp>.

Smith, Adam. Edited by C.J. Bullock. The Wealth of Nations: New York: P.F. Collier Son, 1909–14. Bartleby.com, 2001.

Soderbaum, Dr. Peter, "Post-Autistic Economics Review", Sept 2007

United States Department of Labor. "Youth Employment Rate". February 2013. ODEP. March 2013. http://www.dol.gov/odep/categories/youth/youthemp loyment.htm>.

United States Census Bureau. "The National Data Book". 2012. United States Census Bureau. March 2013. http://www.census.gov/compendia/statab/past_years. html>.

Williamson, Samuel H. "Seven Ways to Compute the Relative Value of a U.S. Dollar Amount, 1774 to present," MeasuringWorth, April 2013. http://www.measuringworth.com/uscompare/index.p hp>.

Wiseman, Paul. "U.S. Productivity Gains Stifle Job Creation". USA Today. April 2011. USA Today. March 2013. http://usatoday30.usatoday.com/money/economy/201 1-04-04-us-economy-jobs.htm>.

Yang, Jia Lynn. "Corporations Pushing for Job-Creation Tax Breaks Shield U.S. vs. Abroad Hiring Data", August 2011. The Washington Post. March

2013.
http://www.washingtonpost.com/business/economy/c
orporations-pushing-for-job-creation-tax-breaks-
shield-us-vs-abroad-hiring-
data/2011/08/12/gIQAZwhqUJ_print.html>.

In Defense of The American System

In Defense of The American System

www.ingramcontent.com/pod-product-compliance
Lightning Source LLC
Chambersburg PA
CBHW061957280526
45787CB00005B/1905